Agents of Social Change

Agents of Social Change

Christian Widows in Northern Nigeria

Sung H. Bauta

Forewords by
Gregg A. Okesson and Theresa Adamu

WIPF & STOCK · Eugene, Oregon

AGENTS OF SOCIAL CHANGE
Christian Widows in Northern Nigeria

Copyright © 2022 Sung H. Bauta. All rights reserved. Except for brief quotations in critical publications or reviews, no part of this book may be reproduced in any manner without prior written permission from the publisher. Write: Permissions, Wipf and Stock Publishers, 199 W. 8th Ave., Suite 3, Eugene, OR 97401.

Wipf & Stock
An Imprint of Wipf and Stock Publishers
199 W. 8th Ave., Suite 3
Eugene, OR 97401

www.wipfandstock.com

PAPERBACK ISBN: 978-1-6667-3837-7
HARDCOVER ISBN: 978-1-6667-9899-9
EBOOK ISBN: 978-1-6667-9900-2

07/12/22

Scripture quotations marked (NIV) are taken from the Holy Bible, New International Version®, NIV®. Copyright © 1973, 1978, 1984, 2011 by Biblica, Inc.™ Used by permission of Zondervan. All rights reserved worldwide. www.zondervan.com. The "NIV" and "New International Version" are trademarks registered in the United States Patent and Trademark Office by Biblica, Inc.™

This book is dedicated to the widows who shared their powerful stories of struggle and faith. Their perseverance amid the many adversities of widowhood is both incentivizing and transformative.

Contents

Foreword by Gregg A. Okesson | ix
Preface by Theresa Adamu | xi
Acknowledgements | xiii
Abbreviations | xv

Introduction | 1

1 Methodological Issues | 14
2 Religion and Agency | 30
3 Religious, Economic and Social Agency | 57
4 Christian Institutions and Agency: A Study of African Pentecostalism | 85
5 A Theological Proposal for Embodied Agency | 110

Conclusions | 141

Bibliography | 149
Index | 159

Foreword

by Gregg A. Okesson

SUNG BAUTA PROVIDES US with an extraordinary gift. This book takes the reader by the hand into the lived experiences of widows in northern Nigeria, listening to their voices, foregrounding their narratives, and painstakingly negotiating their complex daily lives and circumstances.

Rarely does a book offer so much. He begins by telling stories of widows as narrated to him in their contexts. The reader travels with Bauta as he visits different villages throughout Kaduna State, rides with women in his vehicle, attends church with them, enjoys generous hospitality in their homes, and goes out in ministry with them to surrounding NGOs. As Bauta tells their stories, he slowly and gently begins weaving in an incredible array of diverse literatures, including ethnography, inculturation, power, integral mission, African Christianity, and a theology of embodiment, to name a few. Bauta does not overpower their narratives with the literature but nurtures an intimate discourse between written resources and the voices of the widows. It's a compelling symphony of music, sights, sounds, and choreographed movement.

Bauta offers a bold thesis: widows are critical agents of social change in northern Nigeria, and further that they exert holistic agency through religion and with their bodies. Thus, his thesis takes us deeper into themes of development, poverty, structures, embodiment, and theology. It's a wonderful, highly complex case study fed by rich input from African resources.

Foreword

Research of this nature, that deals with such pronounced forms of poverty, tend to foreground the systems, structures, and institutions that perpetuate the marginalization and powerlessness of people. Bauta doesn't pull punches in this book and openly faults the Nigerian government, mainline churches, and other institutions for the ways they have operated according to patriarchy and other structural forms of oppression. However, what makes Bauta's book so compelling is that he doesn't just identify the problems but coaxes institutions themselves into the solution and shows what this looks like with vivid ethnographic description.

At the conclusion of the study the reader leaves with deep appreciation for the collective agency of these women as they navigate tremendous pain, systemic evil, and marginalization. He welcomes us into their worlds, and along the way we learn about the plight of widows, African Christianity, poverty, holistic mission, various NGOs serving in the region, as well as cultural traditions from the region. Any great book or novel has a strong protagonist. Widows in northern Nigeria provide this role. I highly recommend this book.

Wilmore, Kentucky, USA

Foreword
by Theresa Adamu

THIS IS WHERE GOD's heart is—all that concerns the widows and orphans. Other than the work of evangelism and discipleship, nothing stirs the mind of God like the plights of the widow and orphan. As a widow, I have experienced God's concern for widows in formidable ways. As a theologian, I marvel at the ways God uses my challenges to shape the lives of others, especially my students at the seminary.

I do not know what led the author to investigate the agonies of the widow, since he is not a widower or an orphan. Thus, this must be a divine initiative. I am sure the love of God in his heart and the zeal to practice true and pure religion (James 1:27) motivated him to embark on this study. The author understands that the Lord guards and guides the steps of his dearly beloved children such as widows.

This book should find acceptance in the church. The author has dissected the many challenges found amongst African widows today. If a lay person (I mean the author not being an experienced widower or an orphan) could delve into this matter so succinctly, the Lord has a purpose for it.

This book is a living testimony to the clarion call into the mission field of widows and orphans. Some have heeded the call, like the author has pointed out. The mission field—widows—is vast and needs more laborers. With the increase in insecurity and the activities of terrorists in northern Nigeria today, the growing number of widows is alarming! The author cited several institutions who are involved with widows' social and

Foreword

spiritual development in northern Nigeria. But more institutions similar to the existing ones are needed. The churches in northern Nigeria are already overwhelmed with widows and their numerous challenges.

I highly commend the spirit of this masterpiece on widows. The author raises the fine idea of widows as "change agents" in our societies. He mentions that religion or the widow's spiritual faith and standing can influence her mourning rituals (*takaba*), thereby effecting a social and theological change in her society. I like the way the author puts it. Widowhood and mourning rituals are two complex phenomena. You need to read his full submission. He strongly opines for a holistic development of the widow to meet her complex situation.

This work is extensive empirical and literature research embarked upon by the author. It is research that will help the church and society reposition their tasks towards the widow. It is my prayer that Christians will get to read and apply the thoughts outlined herein. This is a "must read" book for church leaders, pastors, politicians, widows, and those in academia.

Jos, Nigeria

Acknowledgments

I THANK THE MANY people who made this book possible. Throughout the research and writing process, Gregg Okesson has been an amazing guide from my doctoral pursuits to today. He has challenged and encouraged me to be the best version of myself.

I also thank Mrs. Jummai Inuwa, the principal at ECWA Widows' School (EWS) at the time of my research, and Mrs. Grace Abbin Yohanna and her colleagues at Ganty's Aid for Widows, Orphans and the Needy (GAWON). They are remarkable leaders who provided tremendous help to me in my field research. I marveled at their incredible leadership at both EWS and GAWON as they inspired and shaped the lives of Christian widows in northern Nigeria.

I thank the independent sources I consulted during the research. It is my hope that the content of this study accurately represents their thoughts. I am thankful to Mrs. Patty Agee, librarian at Central Christian College of the Bible, for getting me the resources I needed to complete this project. Thanks to the people at Milan Christian Church, Missouri. It is a profound privilege to serve you!

Thanks to my dear parents, my siblings, my in-laws, and all my precious nieces and nephews for their love and support. I am grateful to my children: Anaiah, Atarah, and Adinah. Thank you for your patience with me writing and preparing this book for publication. To my amazing wife, Juliet: thank you for your strength and wisdom. It is a privilege to embark

Acknowledgments

on this journey of life with you. Most importantly, nothing is possible without the Lord. To him be all the glory!

Abbreviations

AD	*Anno Domini*
AICs	African Instituted Churches
AIDS	Acquired Immunodeficiency Syndrome
ATR	African Traditional Religion
CBO	Community-Based Organization
CEO	Chief Executive Officer
CIHP	Center for Integrated Health Program
DCC	District Church Council
ECWA	Evangelical Church Winning All
ESSPIN	Education Sector Support Program in Nigeria
EWS	ECWA Widows' School
FCT	Federal Capital Territory
FWC	Family Worship Center
GAWON	Ganty's Aid for Widows, Orphans and the Needy
GDP	Gross Domestic Product
HIV	Human Immunodeficiency Virus

Abbreviations

LGAs	Local Government Areas
NGO	Non-Governmental Organization
OVC	Orphans and Vulnerable Children
RNC	Royal Niger Company

Introduction

It was June 2014. I returned to Nigeria from the US for a summer internship. One of the first things I do whenever I go to Nigeria is to go to our village (an hour from the city of Jos, where my family and I reside) to visit my aged grandparents. I also seize the opportunity to see as many people as possible in the village. In summer 2014, it was my visit to Talata's home that stood out to me. As I entered the house, I realized that her husband was lying down, sick. They lived in a one-bedroom apartment. While age had much to do with her husband's sickness (he was in his late fifties), Talata was only in her late forties.[1] They were very poor. But they were happy to entertain me. All they could afford to offer me was a cup of water to drink. It was heart-wrenching to see their plight. Not too long after my visit, upon my return to the US, the husband died. I kept wondering how she was coping. I was unaware of her plight as a widow until I began researching widows.

---

1. According to the World Factbook of the CIA (CIA, "Nigeria"), estimated life expectancy for a male in Nigeria is fifty years, while that of a female is sixty-three years. Although persistent violence is to blame for the woeful life expectancy in Nigeria, life is especially difficult in northern Nigeria. Economic hardships, for instance, demand intensive labor from the citizens; people work extremely hard to survive. This quickens the aging process as well as the challenges that come with it. Also, as I demonstrate in this study, people in northern Nigeria make up the poorest population of the world. It is also important to note that, like many people in rural Nigeria, Talata and her husband were married quite young, most likely in their late teens or early twenties. In fact, they were already grandparents at the time of our meeting.

Agents of Social Change

In researching widows, I perused several books, articles, blogs, and online videos. Initially, I explored the lives of widows from different contexts before focusing on African widows. I sorted through countless works on widowhood to identify the pertinent literature on widowhood in Africa. I also had conversations with widows and people who worked closely with widows, including church leaders and non-governmental organizations (NGOs). Since I was interested in a biblical theology of widowhood, I studied biblical texts that address the issue of widows. In fact, I wrote papers for a couple of classes that deal with a Christian response to addressing the issue of widowhood in northern Nigeria.

Three years after my encounter with Talata, I returned to northern Nigeria to conduct field research on the plight of Christian widows. Unfortunately, I did not get to see Talata due to ethno-religious violence at the time. She fled to an unknown location for safety. But the widows, administrators, and staff of two organizations informed me of the challenges widows face in northern Nigeria. Because my respondents referred to other organizations that catered to widows, I visited and called those organizations as well.

Consequently, this study provides an engagement between the pertinent literature on widowhood and my conversations with widows and those who work closely with them. What my conversations and the literature revealed to me about Talata and widows like her in northern Nigeria is this: When a woman's husband dies, her in-laws would take the land and any valuable property. If a widow has young children, she might keep the land for the children's sake if her in-laws are reasonable enough to allow that. This arrangement is very rare. If the widow is lucky to have such sensible in-laws, she would keep the land until her in-laws feel the children are old enough for them to take what the community says is rightfully theirs. And where the land goes, the children also go, since the land is supposedly the children's inheritance. But having the land to grow food for her family and following the children to ensure their inheritance means that a widow must embrace levirate marriage, an ancient custom by which a man may be obligated to marry his brother's widow to care for her and her children. Chances are that she and her children would be treated unfairly. Their status would often amount to "slavery," as they would be maltreated by the in-laws who are supposed to care for them. The maltreatment would be largely directed towards the widow to force her out of the family, since she is considered a "burden." In fact, her in-laws would prefer that she leaves the children behind, which exacerbates a widow's feeling of loss and

Introduction

loneliness. In some cases, in-laws have forcefully taken widows' children from them, which intensifies the widow's sense of loss.

If a widow decides to give up the land or any property while choosing to raise her children, she faces another challenge: She has no formal or informal education by which she can get a well-paying job to help her family. Because she was born and raised in her agrarian culture that sees no value in educating women, she has never had any form of education. Moreover, she has lived in the village all her life, and her identity is tied to the land. Thus, to leave the village would be equivalent to social death. But her chances of survival in the village are very slim. Does the widow take her chances and move to the city? And if leaving her children in the village is not an option, how would she move to the city with her children? She would face the inevitable decision of either begging or engaging in prostitution to meet her needs. While begging or prostitution are last resorts, the widow worries that failure in accessing resources would result in her children starving to death.

While narrating her story of severe challenges as a widow, Dominique exclaimed: "Widowhood is a life full of worry. There is nowhere to go. It's worry and worry. You can't eat or sleep due to worry!"[2] What Dominique's statement underscores is the hopelessness that is characteristic of widowhood in northern Nigeria. This hopelessness depicts widows' powerlessness, although I observed that worry is not indicative of lack of confidence in God. In fact, widowhood is becoming for many Christians in northern Nigeria an opportunity for theologizing their lived realities. Dominique states: "Widowhood is not easy. But if one gets tired of it, she hands it over to God. I would pray to God that I am in his hands."[3] And when the widows talked about submission to God's will, there was no sense of fatalism in what they were saying. In fact, it was clear from our conversations that God is the reason that widows hope for a brighter future.

Moreover, Dominique's statement represents the ways widows themselves are demanding theological conversations about empowerment for agency. Widows like Dominique are active members of evangelical churches, where they participate in various church activities such as the *zumunta mata* (women's fellowship group). A major reason for their ecclesiastical participation is due to the strong sense of divine calling that widows like Dominique have. Theresa Adamu, who is twice widowed, has written about her widowhood experiences. As a theologian, Adamu is helping to shape

2. Dominique, interview by author, March 29, 2017.

3. Dominique, interview by author, March 29, 2017.

some of the theological views on widowhood in northern Nigeria. In her book *Widowhood in the 21st Century*, Adamu argues that widowhood is a calling from God.[4] According to Adamu, widowhood is a calling from God because the death of a woman's husband is God's way of calling the woman to depend solely on God rather than on her husband.[5] Also, widowhood is a calling because it is through the death of her husband that God summons a woman to serve him.[6] What Adamu means is that the death of their husbands is the megaphone God uses to inspire Christian widows like Talata and Dominique towards agency. Therefore, widowhood is an "on-the-job" training where the widow perseveres in her faith and utilizes her resources to transform society.

I recall the day I met Dominique. She lived in a compound with two children and a niece. She was a very passionate woman whose hospitality and anecdotes on life as a widow captivated my imagination. But she also captivated the attention of local and international NGOs. She has been receiving help from the local NGO that partners with an international NGO to help widows in northern Nigeria. With the help of these NGOs, Dominique was able to purchase some land and build a befitting home for her family. They have been enjoying their new home for over ten years now. However, their new home has not erased the memories of her widowhood. Memories of her dead husband and three dead children contest every attempt at reframing her current situation. Photos of her once-large family and old family trinkets contribute to an intense nostalgia by which their previous lives are thrust on them daily. These memories, and the other challenges of widowhood, exacerbate Dominique's pain. But she remains resolute in her faith. She expressed a deep sense of confidence in God not only to help her overcome the challenges of widowhood but for God to use her to help others overcome their challenges. Faith thus becomes essential to Dominique's agency.

Therefore, I argue that Christian widows in northern Nigeria are agents of social change, and I outline how. Religion undergirds the lives of Christian widows in northern Nigeria. Because religion undergirds their lives, I demonstrate that the widows' Christian faith enhances their religious, social, and economic agency. Further, Christian institutions best guide their embodied agency. And I frame my theory of embodiment by

---

4. Adamu, *Widowhood in the 21st Century*.
5. Adamu, *Widowhood in the 21st Century*, 19.
6. Adamu, *Widowhood in the 21st Century*, 51.

considering how Christian widows embody the ways mourning rituals will lead to social change in northern Nigeria.

I offer this study as a hybrid between empirically-driven data and library research-based data. Therefore, arguing that Christian widows in northern Nigeria effect social change draws upon both my empirical data and the diverse literature on widows within Africa. In fact, I frame the concept of embodiment from an integrative theology-social science literature hybrid. This approach is based on the evidence from the literature on African widows and my empirical data. As this study shows, there is a need to integrate the social and theological to enhance how Christian widows can embody the ways mourning rituals will lead to social change in northern Nigeria. I suggest that embodiment aids in investigating and analyzing how Christian widows in northern Nigeria can be agents of social change. I approach embodiment in this study from a Christian theological perspective.

Several pertinent themes emerge from Christian embodiment that need to be highlighted. These themes will be at the backdrop of this study. The themes of embodiment I draw upon include a holistic approach to development, inculturation, and the interaction of religion and social change in northern Nigeria. What makes these themes compelling is that they engage the conversation between the social science and theology. These themes help in investigating how Christian widows can embody the ways mourning rituals will lead to social change within their specific contexts, how developing widows' lives involves addressing the holistic needs of society, and how religion can be a tool towards social change.

Embodiment in Northern Nigeria

Embodiment refers to an idea or feeling that assumes a tangible form.[7] Christian widows in northern Nigeria can embody the idea of a brighter future for northern Nigeria. Moreover, women in northern Nigeria are embodied all the time. And their embodiment is a part of religion in northern Nigeria. In fact, African embodiment is inseparable from religion.[8] Religion is the basis for these women's embodied agency. Women in northern Nigeria embody their religious convictions in their roles as wives, mothers, and citizens. By performing these roles, they also embody the rituals associated with womanhood. This means that they perform their culturally

7. Allegranti, *Embodied Performances*, 2.
8. Tanabe, "African Philosophy."

sanctioned roles as wives, mothers, and citizens of northern Nigeria. Their religious convictions authenticate these rituals of womanhood by positioning African women to effect social change.

As with the rituals of womanhood, religion also authenticates the mourning rituals that widows undergo. Consequently, I suggest that Christian widows can embody the ways mourning ritual, a religiously sanctioned procedure for widows in northern Nigeria, will lead towards social change. In other words, the purpose of embodiment is to portray the ways that widows' mourning rituals will lead to social change. Thus, I portray the mourning rituals in symbolic forms to propose a theology of embodiment that leads to social change. In his salient work on African rituals, Victor Turner's book *The Ritual Process* explores the rituals of the Ndembu in Zambia and formulates the notion of "communitas."[9] He attributes it to an absolute inter-human relation that exceeds any type of structure. Turner shows that the analysis of ritual behavior and symbolism can be crucial to comprehending social structures and processes. He extends anthropologist Arnold van Gennep's idea of the "liminal phase" of rites of passage to an extensive stage and applies it to obtain an understanding of complex social phenomena such as widowhood.[10]

What Turner's book demonstrates is that rituals have become central arenas towards social change. Therefore, I suggest that Christian widows in northern Nigeria can embody the ways mourning rituals will lead to social change. Because widowhood is a complex social phenomenon, mourning rituals are means toward addressing the complex realities of widowhood and articulating widows' embodied agency. Rituals enhance a broadening vision that takes widows' lived realities into account. In northern Nigeria, rituals ensure that a holistic approach to development is pertinent for embodiment. Specifically, a holistic approach to widows' development ensures that Christian widows can embody the ways mourning rituals lead to social change.

---

9. Turner, *Ritual Process*.

10. Arnold van Gannep is best known for his studies of the rites of passage in various cultures. His major work is *The Rites of Passage* (1909), where he compares ceremonies celebrating a person's transition from one status to another in a society. He observed three phases/stages in the liminal process: separation, transition, and reincorporation.

Introduction
Holistic Approach to Development

A holistic approach to developing widows' lives is vital for an embodied agency that leads towards social change. Therefore, I demonstrate in this book that embodiment involves appropriating Western and African motifs[11] to meet societal needs.[12] By "appropriating," I mean the ways widows draw upon Western and African motifs towards social change. In chapter 4, I suggest that Pentecostalism as an institution best guides the agency of Christian widows towards social change in northern Nigeria. Pentecostalism's effectiveness at guiding widows' agency feeds into the conversation I broker in chapter 5 between African sociology and theology for Christian widows to use holistic approach to development towards embodying the ways mourning rituals will lead to social change.

D. E. Miller and T. Yamamori state that foundational to the effective measures Pentecostalism uses in engendering the embodied agency of women is the holistic approach to ministry.[13] In her article "Going and Making Public," Birgit Meyer states that Pentecostalism is a public religion that demands taking seriously the material, tangible dimensions of life.[14] According to Meyer, this necessitates a review of the conventional view that dichotomizes between religion and social realities. Meyer suggests the need to rethink the public sphere by rejecting Western dualisms that stem from idealist and elitist perspective. Rethinking the public space requires embracing African (and even Western) holism that encourages the interaction between the public and the private. Pentecostalism demands public and private interactions. Meyer researched African appropriations of Christianity and the appeal of Pentecostalism in Ghana, observing that one of Pentecostalism's appeals is its engagement with the public sphere.[15] Therefore, Meyer suggests discovering Christian appropriations and Pentecostalism's appeal as she calls for an interaction between the public sphere and religious institutions. Such an interaction can help towards envisioning new paths where the widows embody the ways mourning rituals will lead to social change.

---

11. By "motifs," I am referring to Western and African economic, social, and religious realities.

12. Hadisi, "Exploring," 443–53.

13. See Miller and Yamamori, *Global Pentecostalism*; see also Freeman, "The Pentecostal Ethic," 1–40.

14. Meyer, "Going and Making Public."

15. Meyer, "Going and Making Public," 150.

Agents of Social Change

There are further implications of the interaction between the public and private. A holistic approach to development ensures widows' complex needs are not only met, but it also enhances the embodied agency of widows. In other words, widows are positioned to embody the ways mourning rituals will lead to social change. Most mainline churches in northern Nigeria which provide a wide array of social services are becoming ineffective because they limit their focus to just economic empowerment. To focus largely on economic empowerment of the widow is to pursue a failed empowering agenda that is pertinent to widows' embodied agency. The widows need more than just financial support; they require an approach to empowerment that takes all aspects of their lives into consideration to ensure that widows' agency is holistic in nature.

The failure of most mainline churches in northern Nigeria towards a holistic approach to development of widows is because the structural power of these mainline churches tends to operate patriarchally, which hinders the full participation of widows. This follows the dualistic pattern, which endorses the stereotypical roles that limit widows' participation. Pentecostalism allows the input of women into its institutional forms because Pentecostalism's holistic approach to development demands women's participation in social reforms. And this is because Pentecostalism promotes the interaction between the public and private, which positions widows to embody the ways mourning rituals will lead to social change.

In chapter 4, I expound on how Pentecostalism uses a holistic approach to development to engender the agency of widows. Then, in chapter, 5, I show how widows can use a holistic approach to development in embodying the ways mourning rituals will lead to social change by mediating the power of Jesus' incarnation. Meanwhile, another theme of embodiment is inculturation. What that suggests is that embodied agency requires empowering widows to effect changes within their local contexts. In other words, embodiment for Christian widows in northern Nigeria involves making their agency relevant to specific contexts.

Introduction

Inculturation[16]

In his article "Critical Contextualization," anthropologist Paul Hiebert argues for presenting the gospel in a culturally relevant way.[17] In short, contextualization or inculturation is the process by which the gospel takes root in a specific socio-cultural context. In his book *The Inculturation of Christianity in Africa*, Joseph Osei-Bonsu reveals the outcomes that the interaction between Christianity and African cultures is creating for African Christians.[18] Drawing attention to peculiar traditional African beliefs and practices that seem to be incompatible with Christianity, Osei-Bonsu suggests the need for the inculturation of Christianity in Africa.

Osei-Bonsu suggests seven guidelines to engage in the exercise of inculturation.[19] However, I narrow it down to Hiebert's more generic four stages of contextualization because Osei-Bonsu's other three guidelines are specific to his context. First, we must analyze the context. This involves comprehending the facts, meanings, and values of the village or town in which Christian widows find themselves. It means figuring out elements in the culture that Christian widows can use to effect social change. This stage is critical to the process of embodiment because it demands Christian widows evaluate traditional rituals that affect people's lives, including their own lives. Second, Christian widows need to apply Scripture to the context. Scripture must be the point of departure for the process of inculturation. D. A. Carson argues that faithful contextualized theology must be grounded in the entire Bible.[20] In my analysis, I demonstrate how embodying mourning rituals towards social change within northern Nigeria is grounded in the Bible.

Third, Christian widows must critically select elements within their specific contexts. In other words, widows must recognize the positive and negative aspects of cultural values. My assumption is that their biblical foundation would enable them to discard cultural elements that conflict with Christian values. At the same time, they embrace elements of culture they can reapply to embody the ways mourning rituals will lead to social change. Finally, the goal is that as Christian widows bring the public and

16. This word is known by several names, which include "contextualization" and "indigenization."
17. Hiebert, "Critical Contextualization," 104–11.
18. Osei-Bonsu, *Inculturation of Christianity*.
19. Osei-Bonsu, *Inculturation of Christianity*, 119.
20. Carson, "Reflections on Contextualization," 51.

private spheres of their faith and cultures together, Christian values would transform and reshape the cultural practices such as mourning rituals towards new realities that engender social change. In chapter 5, I show how widows use inculturation towards embodying the ways mourning rituals will lead to social change by mediating the power of Jesus' incarnation.

The description of embodiment and inculturation is critical in developing my thoughts on the embodied agency of Christians widows in northern Nigeria. Particularly, embodiment and inculturation highlight the concept of "gaze." What I mean is that embodiment involves the idea of being "seen" as one lives out the power of Jesus' incarnation in a culturally relevant way. Embodied agency of Christian widows requires societal gaze, recognition that widows have the potential to contribute towards social change. In the conclusion of this study, I describe empowering widows for agency through the lens of gaze. But I turn now to discussing the pertinent interrelation between religion and social change. This is another pertinent element of embodiment because it underscores the interplay between religion and the social science, an interaction that is pertinent to this study.

Religion and Social Change

I describe religion and social change together because my empirical research and the literature research show a strong link between these themes. Social change involves changes in nature, social institutions, social behaviors, or social relations. There are many theories of social change, but the focus of this study is on the current social changes of gendered patterns of work and care. This involves the modifications of gender roles, where the need for embodied agency is emphasized. Social change in Africa has been examined from anthropological, sociological, theological, political, and economic viewpoints. Among the major issues these diverse disciplines focus on are the changing statuses of women and the many modern types of organizations which involve the influence that religion such as Christianity is having on the African way of life.[21] Theologians such as Emmanuel Katongole draw from sociological works to advocate for social change within Africa.[22] In fact, Katongole locates the conversation on social change within African religious sentiments because religion is central to Africans. Several

21. Eisenstadt, "Social Change," 453–71.
22. Katongole, *Future for Africa*.

Introduction

literatures underscore the central role religion plays in the lives of Africans. I draw upon some of the literature in this study.

Due to the centrality of religion in the African consciousness, social developments possess a religious character. In the book *Development and Politics from Below*, the editors argue that religion is assuming an ever-expanding critical role in African political and developmental existence.[23] Therefore, the writers offer both empirical and theoretical reflections on the connection between religion, politics, and development in Africa; the book also provides the meanings of religion in non-Western contexts and the way that religion is inserted in the everyday life of people in Africa. Religion has a pertinent role to play in social change within northern Nigeria. As I noted above, widows' embodiment is a part of their religious convictions. Religion's correlation to embodied agency leads to social change. I should note that the widows understand that the social change that is brokered by religion is not easily managed or reversed; however, their conviction about the role of religion towards social change is resolute. Christian widows recognize that religion can effect either positive or negative social changes in society, but it does not prevent them from integrating their faith within their lived experiences towards social change. Because this study is a hybrid between the theological and social sciences, I demonstrate the ways widows use religion and social change towards embodied agency. Therefore, what I propose is an embodiment that stems from the interaction between religion and social change.

Plan of the Book

The challenges of widowhood and the resources of the Christian faith to engender agency in widows[24] are the two central themes to be investigated throughout this study. To provide a robust understanding of the complexity surrounding widowhood in northern Nigeria, I examine the dynamics of religion, particularly the way Christian faith shapes the social realities of widowhood in northern Nigeria.[25] Thus, each chapter examines the ways

---

23. Bompani and Frahm-Arp, *Development and Politics*.

24. In this study, the terms "Christian widow" and "widow" will be used interchangeably. There are also times when I use the generic expression "African woman" to refer to women of status, including widows.

25. Unless otherwise stated, I will use the terms "religion," "faith," and "Christianity" interchangeably in this study. The widows did not differentiate between any these terms

that religion or faith influences the agency of widows in northern Nigeria, although the chapters mutually reinforce one another in several ways. I explore the ways that Christian widows in northern Nigeria are agents of social change.

In chapter 1, I present my methodology. I state the problem of this study and present the research questions to address the research problem. Next, I describe the two organizations in which I conducted my field research. I discuss the use of ethnographic interviews, the respondents for the research, how ethnography relates to literature, and the delimitations and significance of this study.

In chapter 2, I argue that religion undergirds the agency of Christian widows in northern Nigeria. I establish the important correlation between religion and widows' agency in northern Nigeria by demonstrating that northern Nigeria's history consists of religious antecedents that influence the lives of Christian widows from their marital homes to their widowhood. This leads into conversation about how the interaction between religion and social change represents the combination of local rituals and Christian rites. Consequently, I conclude by demonstrating the important role Christianity plays towards the widows' agency.

In chapter 3, I argue that faith engenders greater religious, economic, and social agency towards social change. I demonstrate what the widows have accomplished towards social change in northern Nigeria. Then, I explore how faith enhances greater achievements for widows by addressing the issue of "status." I suggest that the widows' roles as wives and mothers position widows to effect social change. What I demonstrate is that widows' agency arises from limited religious, economic, and social resources that are characteristic of widowhood.

In chapter 4, I argue that Christian institutions best guide the agency of Christian widows in northern Nigeria. I describe the social institutions in northern Nigeria as I show the pertinent role religion plays in guiding widows' agency. I provide a brief historical background on how Christian institutions became central to development initiatives in Africa. Then, I examine how Pentecostalism in its institutional form guides the agency of people in northern Nigeria. Finally, I suggest two pertinent ways that Pentecostalism effectively guides the agency of widows in northern Nigeria.

In chapter 5, I argue that widows can embody the ways mourning rituals *will* lead to social change by mediating the power of Jesus'

---

because they have a holistic worldview of how God operates in the world.

Introduction

incarnation. Integrating the previous chapters, I propose a theology of embodiment that demonstrates what Christian widows could do with agency. I weave a conversation between Ola Sigurdson and feminist theologians to show the link between embodiment and incarnation that engenders social change. Then, I show that widows are using Christianity and social change, holistic approaches to development, and inculturation to embody the ways mourning rituals will lead to social change by mediating the power of Jesus' incarnation.

And, in the conclusion, I summarize my arguments in this study. I do so by considering empowering widows for agency through the concept of gaze.

1

Methodological Issues

BECAUSE THIS STUDY IS located at the junction between social and theological analyses, it calls on both disciplinary frameworks to bolster and inform one another. Nicholas Adams and Charles Elliott state that it is the purpose of theology to teach Christians to embrace a vision that leads towards transformation.[1] In other words, an embodied theology must consider and seek to transform the social realities around it. I should note that in this study, "theology" will refer to the ritual processes of faith and practices and the theological reflections that people's faith and practices initiate. In northern Nigeria, theology is both abstract and concrete. Theology involves a set of propositions about God, but theology is also about establishing a link between God and people. This theologizing happens in pertinent locations where people share their faith and experiences. For Christian widows in northern Nigeria, their theologizing involves how their Christian faith might engender their agency within a context that provides them with no power.

In my goal to explore how to empower Christian widows for social change in northern Nigeria, this chapter states the problem of this study. Then, I present the research questions to address the research problem. Next, I describe the two organizations in which I conducted my field research. In describing my methodology, I discuss the use of ethnographic

---

1. Adams and Elliott, "Ethnography," 364.

Methodological Issues

interviews, the respondents for the research, how ethnography relates to literature, and the delimitations and significance of this study.

Marginalization and Disempowerment

As noted in the introduction, Dominique's hopelessness represents the powerlessness that is characteristic of widowhood in northern Nigeria. Widows in northern Nigeria have no power. Therefore, widows in northern Nigeria face grave challenges towards agency. Margaret Owen, a leading figure in the emerging widows' rights movement, states that widows in sub-Saharan Africa are generally the poorest of the poor and the least protected by the law.[2] Owen also points out that widowhood represents a "social death for women, robbing them of their status and consigning them to the very margins of society where they suffer the most extreme forms of discrimination and stigma."[3] There is a sizeable body of literature to demonstrate the fact that Nigerian widows are indeed marginalized and stigmatized, routinely discriminated against in a variety of ways, and frequently encounter varying degrees of economic hardships.[4]

Christian widows in northern Nigeria are disempowered economically. Without land, education, and marketable skills, they have no way to provide for their families or even contribute towards social reforms. But they are also disempowered socially and religiously. Because widowhood demands isolation, widows are forced to abdicate the relationships within which they thrive. What is worse, religion becomes a tool that perpetuates their marginalization in every dimension of life. I say "worse" because religion undergirds widows' lives in northern Nigeria; unfortunately, religion is used to further disempower widows. Leanne M. Dzubinski provides a comparison of social gender role stereotypes with evangelical gender roles.[5] One distinguishing feature within gender roles is the assertion that men are "agentic" and women are "communal."[6] The former refers to a person who rejects the idea that they are reactive organisms shaped by environmental

---

2. Owen, "Widows in Third World Nations."

3. Owen, "Widows in Third World Nations."

4. Iwobi, "No Cause for Merriment," 38. Cf. Omoregbe, "Perspectives," 83; Enemo, "Widowhood and Property Inheritance," 290; Rotimi, "Paradox of 'Progress,'" 137; Ibhawoh, *Culture and Constitution*, 44.

5. Dzubinski, "Taking on Power," 283.

6. Dzubinski, "Taking on Power," 282.

forces or driven by inner impulse, while the latter refers to a person who depends on the community to define their identity and approve actions. Consequently, when women use agentic behaviors to accomplish their responsibilities, they encounter disapproval.[7] Therefore, they continue to suffer marginalization and disempowerment.

Ways to Empower Christian Widows

To investigate how to empower Christian widows for social change in northern Nigeria, I pursued three research questions. First, what roles, if any, are Christian widows currently playing in northern Nigeria? Second, what social networks/institutions guide the agency of widows in relation to northern Nigeria? And third, how do their social statuses enhance their role as agents of social change in northern Nigeria?

These research questions relate to the study in two ways. First, these research questions help to unravel the multilayered ways that religion undergirds the lives of Christian widows in northern Nigeria. And second, the research questions also provide themes necessary to describe the interaction between religion and widowhood in northern Nigeria. Specifically, these questions contribute to my proposal that widows are agents for social change in northern Nigeria. To explore these questions, I researched two organizations in northern Nigeria: ECWA Widows' School (EWS) and Ganty's Aid for Widows, Orphans and the Needy (GAWON) Foundation. I provide background, context, and comparisons of these two organizations below.

ECWA Widows' School (EWS)

The Nigerian civil war lasted from 1967 to 1970. By its end, over one million people had died. Many of those who died were men, leaving behind their wives and children. Mrs. Chidawa Kaburuk, the wife of an Evangelical Church Winning All (ECWA) church leader, suggested that the leadership of seven Women Fellowship of Eastern Zaria District Church Councils (DCCs) help these widows. This led to the birth of the Women Craft School in April 1979.

---

7. Dzubinski, "Taking on Power," 282.

Methodological Issues

Nestled in the rural village of Samaru Kataf, Kaduna, the Women Craft School (now ECWA Widows' School) offers courses in sewing, cooking, and biblical knowledge. Initially, the school depended on the donations of institutions, organizations, and individuals within Nigeria to operate; those donations came in the form of sewing machines, cooking utensils, ingredients, Bibles, and other learning materials. The women's fellowship groups of the seven DCCs contributed their monies and devoted their time to ensuring the sustainability of the school.

The ECWA Widow School, hereafter EWS, was established with the aim of helping widows and women cater for themselves and their children and to create a chance for re-marriage for those who wish to re-marry.[8] Joseph Bagaiya Awans presents the objectives of the EWS.[9] First, EWS trains widows with the aim of rehabilitating and providing functional education for them; second, EWS aims to contribute to nation-building in Nigeria; and, third, EWS seeks to train widows to be able to earn their living and maintain their families without much difficulty.[10]

The school's overarching objective is to help the widow (re)discover her purpose. Two major areas indicate this goal. First, when the school began operations in 1979, it had five people on staff, with three being women and two being men. One of the three women, Deborah Bonat, was the principal.[11] This proved monumental because her position as principal legitimized the widows' plights and inspired their agency. Both ECWA and the school realized that empowering these widows requires a cultural shift regarding its view of women in leadership positions. Bonat's appeal for the widows was further enhanced when her husband died while she was principal. She assumed a position in the hearts of the widows in ways that none of the male counterparts could. Bonat's twenty years as principal helped tremendously in establishing the school's prominence, especially in northern Nigeria. Bonat's success paved the way for successive female administrators of the school for the unforeseeable future. In fact, the management of the school is overwhelmingly female today. Several widows pointed to these female administrators and teachers as their inspirations for overcoming the challenges of widowhood.

8. Inuwa, *ECWA Widow's School Happenings*.
9. Awans, "Analysis of the Objectives," 6.
10. Awans, "Analysis of the Objectives," 37.
11. She was still married when she assumed the position. This ties into the third point regarding the school's decision at the time to admit married women.

Second, of the women from the first graduation, half of them were currently married at the time of enrollment, and some of them were single women who had never married. The reason for admitting non-widows into the school was not just to boost enrollment, but because the school reasoned that every married woman was a potential widow.[12] This might seem very fatalistic to some, but two reasons justify this rationale: (1) There are married women in northern Nigeria who describe themselves as "widows" because their husbands refuse to fulfill their roles. Thus, the EWS continued to admit both married women and even single women. One widow who joined the school before her husband's death said what she learned at the widows' school helped her to assume her dual roles before his death. In other words, she realized she did not need her husband to thrive. And (2) Globally, men die earlier than women. This is especially true in northern Nigeria.

In sum, the school has maintained its vision of helping the widows who lived in their communities by inspiring their agency in society. EWS maintains its objectives of biblical training and skills acquisition to ensure that this is achieved. In chapter 3, I demonstrate the relationship between their biblical training and the social services widows receive. GAWON Foundation shares some characteristics with EWS and possesses some unique features as well.

GAWON Foundation

GAWON Foundation is a community-based organization (CBO) that is non-governmental,[13] non-profitmaking, and non-partisan. Founded in 1998 by Elder Takai A. Shamang, who is also the president and CEO, GAWON focuses on empowering widows, while also catering to orphans and vulnerable children (OVC) and other vulnerable / less privileged groups in the society. Its vision statement read, "Making fortune out of misfortune." Shamang classifies widows into three: a widow whose husband left her with material wealth, a widow who is educated enough to secure a well-paying job, and a widow who has neither material wealth nor education.[14] He said the mission of "replacing tears of sorrow with tears of joy" involves doing everything necessary to empower the third category of widows.

12. Awans, "Analysis of the Objectives," 40.

13. It is fair to say that GAWON fits the description of a faith-based organization than an NGO. As I show in this study, faith is integral in the management of the organization.

14. Takai A. Shamang, interview by author, March 27, 2017.

Methodological Issues

To achieve its mission, GAWON focuses on two major areas: agriculture and education. First, GAWON is involved in agriculture such as animal husbandry, aquaculture, crop farming, cash crops, root crops, and plantation. GAWON's machinery service aids farmers in transporting farming equipment. This is especially important for widows who need help with some of the heavy farming equipment. GAWON also provides seeds for the widows during planting season.

Second, due to the high demand of comprehensive OVC services particularly and educational support in and around GAWON's immediate community, GAWON runs a free private nursery and primary school. GAWON manages over eleven cooperative societies, including a computer programming skills acquisition program, which are activities aimed at strengthening households economically. GAWON provides capacity building, which largely involves HIV counseling and testing; the organization connects widows with hospitals and clinics to address their health challenges. And, finally, GAWON provides psychosocial support, which includes providing guidance and counseling and reconciling families and communities.

These agricultural and educational ventures serve to bring the widows' communities together. The aim is that by participating in agricultural and educational ventures, the community will come to see the value of all its citizens, including the widows. For the widows, these ventures are meant to provide them with the skills they need to thrive. Moreover, through farming and education, GAWON provides the widow (and even her children) the opportunity to participate in transforming her community.

An important theme for this study is religion. Therefore, I need to state that there is a religious component to GAWON. This will be evident in some of the responses provided in this study. Because its reach includes both Muslims and Christians, GAWON is not very "vocal" about its religious standing; however, it is founded and led by Christians. They operate within biblical principles and have people who provide the spiritual guidance that its administrators, staff, and widows need. I participated in a few worship services organized by GAWON.

Their target groups in these communities include vulnerable children and their caregivers, children at school, school dropouts, parents, community leaders and stakeholders, women, pregnant women, youths, and elderly people. GAWON works with both national (i.e., state, and local government officials, churches, other NGOs) and international partners such as STEER Incorporated; they also utilize programs such as ESSPIN (Education Sector Support Program in Nigeria), and CIHP (Center for Integrated Health Program) in response to the plight of marginalized groups such as widows.

By being in the community offering help to widows, GAWON can determine how society perceives the widows.[15] This enables GAWON to know how best to help the widow discover her agency in society. Also, being present in the community gives GAWON the opportunity to educate the community on the agency of widows.

GAWON and EWS: A Comparison

I selected EWS and GAWON because they provide two important lenses into the diverse Christian efforts of widow empowerment. They share some significant points of similarities. First, they are both founded and managed by Christians. Second, the Evangelical Church Winning All (ECWA),[16] the proprietor of EWS, has a significant presence in northern Nigeria, and GAWON's presence is also in northern Nigeria. Third, the main objective of EWS and GAWON is to cater primarily to widows, although they provide some services to orphans and other needy people in their communities. And, lastly, they are both located in the northern Nigerian state of Kaduna.

But EWS and GAWON also have unique differences that made for fascinating research. First, the EWS is managed by ECWA, while GAWON is operated by an NGO. EWS adheres to more strict rules established by ECWA, which includes providing services only to Christians, but GAWON operates on a more flexible program which allows it to serve both Christians and Muslims. Second, EWS has the characteristic of an educational institution guided by a curriculum, while GAWON does not have a rigid structure for the widows. Next, the widows at EWS have vacations, so there are significant periods when they are not on the school's premises, while the widows at GAWON are catered to year-round. These organizations

---

15. Different caseworkers are assigned to widows in certain parts of the community. These caseworkers go to the widows to evaluate their progress and address any challenges they might have. Some of their challenges range from health, financial, and legal troubles. It is the caseworker's responsibility to report their findings and work with the management to determine how best to address them.

16. ECWA is the largest protestant denomination in northern Nigeria. ECWA boasts of over six million members and has thousands of local churches across Nigeria.

provide services they believe best empower widows in northern Nigeria, particularly in Kaduna State.

Kaduna State is unique for a couple of reasons. First, Kaduna State is a unique state in the predominantly Muslim region of northern Nigeria; it is not only the third largest state in Nigeria (with approximately nine million people), but also the second largest state in northern Nigeria after Kano State. And second, Kaduna is more religiously diverse than Kano State, as it has significant number of Christians and Muslims. In fact, the British colonizers made Kaduna the capital of the northern region in 1916 because of Kaduna's strategic location.

All of Nigeria's thirty-six states are made up of local government areas (LGAs), the arm of the government that reaches the people in the remote parts of the country. Kaduna State has twenty-three local government areas. EWS is in Zangon-Kataf LGA, while GAWON has its presence in three LGAs: Jaba, Jema'a, Kaura, and Zangon-Kataf.[17] This made collecting data quite an adventure; however, it enabled me to interact with several people connected with the two organizations to comprehend the lived realities of widows.

Now I describe the process of collecting and analyzing the data from my respondents in these organizations. I collected data from the local government areas where these organizations had their presence. Again, this enabled me to reach a wider segment of my respondents for a broader perspective on the lives of widows.

Data Collection and Analysis

This study required combining qualitative data and theological forms. I have already described some aspects of the theological method above, and I will say more about it since this study is an interaction between the social and the theological. Thus, it is the qualitative methods that are outlined below.

---

17. These LGAs are in the region known as "Southern Kaduna," a predominantly Christian part of Muslim-dominated Kaduna State.

Respondents

The respondents were selected based on their ability to inform the research questions and to enhance understanding of the phenomenon under study.[18] This was ascertained during the period of initial observations and through the "gatekeepers" at the research sites. These gatekeepers were respected widows and individuals working with the widows; they introduced me to administrators, staff, and widows who became my respondents for this research. All the respondents were ethnic Nigerians who had been widowed or have worked extensively with widows. Other respondents included pastors, elders, and fellowship group leaders where most of the widows were members or attend services and other NGOs that serve widows in northern Nigeria. Every respondent identified themselves as a Christian (except patrons of one of the other NGOs, who said they adhered to no faith). At the time of my research, the respondents were all living in Kaduna State where they attend/work at either EWS or GAWON.

Instrument

H. Russell Bernard writes, "Unstructured interviewing goes on all the time and just about anywhere."[19] There were unstructured questions for the respondents. However, there were semi-structured questions that guided my conversations with the respondents. Both unstructured and semi-structured questions were open-ended. These open-ended personal interviews followed a more narrative approach, where I allowed the respondents, particularly the widows, to tell their stories.[20] The interviews occurred in the offices of the administrators and staff, at the homes of administrators and widows, at shops, markets, classrooms, churches, and on farms. The interviews were in English and Hausa (the dominant regional language of northern Nigeria). The conversations were recorded, transcribed, and analyzed.

---

18. Kuper, Lingard, and Levinson, "Critically Appraising Qualitative Research," 1035.
19. Bernard, *Research Methods*, 211.
20. Spradley, *Participant Observation*, 34–35.

Methodological Issues

Procedure

Before describing the procedure used in collecting data, I should note that, as a researcher, I am both an insider and an outsider. I am an "insider" because I am a Nigerian; specifically, I am from northern Nigeria. I am also from a village where the widow practices I described above occur. But I am an "outsider" because as an African male, society demands distance between genders; thus, my understanding of the African woman is limited. Moreover, my understanding of African widows is even more limited, since society demands that they live in isolation from the rest of society. Other than gender, I am an "insider" because I have participated in some widow empowerment initiatives, which gives me some knowledge of the widows' predicaments. However, I am an "outsider" because my socio-economic status differs from that of the widows; they are poor, but I belong to the Nigerian middle class. Socially, I am an "insider" because I have closely interacted with widows through the widowhood initiative I mention in chapter 2; we share a few things in common, most notably our desire for a better Nigeria. However, we differ in several ways. First, my educational accomplishments (two masters and a doctorate degree) put me in an elite class. Most of these widows have no formal education, while some of them have very little informal education. Second, I am not only more educated than they are, but I have a Western education, which is a distinguishing mark across Nigeria. Third, due to my father's service to the Nigerian society and his leadership roles at the highest levels of ECWA, my status is enhanced by the recognition he also receives.

Therefore, I approached this research recognizing the need to subvert many of my preconceived ideas about widowhood. I recruited the respondents through the gatekeepers I had contacted prior to my arrival at my research sites. Upon my arrival, I met with the gatekeepers to discuss my research needs. Once we established what my research objectives were, they recommended the people I needed to interview and observe. As an outsider, this ensured my credibility, particularly among the widows. Because authentic relationship is important to the widows, the relationship I was able to have with the gatekeepers gave the widows some ease about my presence.

Agents of Social Change

Analytic Framework (Data Analysis)

Data analysis took into consideration all the relevant available evidence from the data, including all major rival interpretations. And findings were interpreted and presented using a narrative analysis. Thus, the focus was on the life story of the people, especially the widows.

Narrative analysis is a method of qualitative research in which the researcher listens to the stories of the research subjects, attempting to understand the relationships between the experiences of the individuals and their social framework. Therefore, I used Jerome Bruner's functional approach.[21] A functional approach to narrative analysis focuses on the way that the narrative enables individuals make sense of their lives, specifically through shaping arbitrary and chaotic events into a coherent narrative that makes the events easier to handle by giving them meaning. Basically, functional approach to narrative analysis focuses on the roles that narratives serve for different individuals. By this model: (1) the narratives were viewed based on how individuals constructed and made sense of the realities of widowhood; (2) the narratives were also viewed by how individuals created and shared meanings of the widows' lived experiences. In short, functional approach to narrative analysis focuses on the interpretations of events related in the narratives by the individuals telling their stories.

I interpreted the data by synthesizing both a feminist and ethnic paradigm based on embodied process. This form of theory was critical, historical, and came from the standpoint of the participants. In short, this type of narration came mainly from the stories of the participants.

I used open coding and axial coding and created a table to analyze the data. In open coding, I looked at distinct concepts and categories in the data; these formed the basic units of my analysis. This involved breaking the data into master headings and/or subheadings. In axial coding, I used the concepts and categories as I re-read the text to (a) ascertain that the concepts and categories accurately represented interview responses, and (b) explore how the concepts and categories are related. To achieve this, I asked questions such as, "What conditions influenced the concepts and categories?" and "What are the associated effects?" Finally, I transferred final concepts into a data table. The research lists the major categories and explains them after the table. The major themes include religion, agency, institution, and embodiment.

21. Bruner, *Acts of Meaning*.

Methodological Issues

The themes of religion, agency, institution, and embodiment were chosen because: (1) Every respondent referred to each theme explicitly and implicitly; (2) These themes give us a vantage point of where religious credence and praxis can be observed before and during widowhood; and (3) due to their importance in widowhood, these themes represent the rationale for widowhood practices since they were contested and tended to highlight the tensions and perils characteristic of widowhood experiences.

The theme of "religion" refers to the Christian faith, although Islam, the major religion in northern Nigeria, is also in the background. Religion is the foundational issue to be negotiated regarding widowhood since religion locates every other discourse related to widowhood, including agency, institution, and embodiment. Thus, without religion, other themes on developing widows' lives cannot be adequately explored. In short, religion is the medium through which the widow hopes to be empowered to transform society, although she recognizes the path towards agency is riddled with many challenges. In chapter 2, I demonstrate that religion undergirds the context of northern Nigeria, and thus the lives of widows in northern Nigeria.

The second theme is "agency." This characterized the widowhood experience. The emotion behind losing one's husband and the ways widows negotiate the loss of their husbands is the basis of chapter 3. Like religion, the respondents referred to agency as a primary theme where widowhood was experienced daily. In chapter 3, I describe the way that faith informs the economic, social, and religious agency of Christian widows in northern Nigeria.

The third theme is "institution." For this research, the institutions I consider are Christian institutions (i.e., churches, hospitals, schools, banks, and NGOs) that aim to empower people towards agency. Based on their evangelical convictions, the widows overwhelmingly noted that they consider Christian institutions central to their empowerment that leads to social change. In chapter 4, I explore ways that Christian institutions best guide the agency of Christian widows in northern Nigeria.

The last theme in the interview is the widows' "embodiment." Based on the respondents and my observations, widows' bodies are contested because of the restrictions of religion. Bodies are particularly important with regards to Christian religious practices during evangelical Christian worship and are principal locations for how to comprehend the way evangelical Christians negotiate the constraint on embodied agency. This is the subject matter of chapter 5, where I recommend a theology of embodiment that can lead to social change.

These themes become pertinent in the interaction between empirical research and library research. As I noted earlier, this study is a hybrid between empirical research and library research. Therefore, my methodology is the integration of theology and social science. During my analyzing of the data, I came across several places where the empirical data and the literature provided fascinating interactions. Based on the four themes I pursue in this study, I describe the interrelationship between the empirical research and literature in four distinct ways.

Empirical and Literature Research

First, the empirical data and literature address the important role that religion plays in the lives of Christian widows in northern Nigeria. The response from the widows overwhelmingly suggests the role religion plays in their lives. All the widows acknowledged the Lord in their heartwrenching stories. They attributed their widowhood to "God's grace." The pertinent role of religion for these African widows aligns with the positions of most of the literature. In fact, the literature demonstrates that African women will resist any form of social change if it undermines their religious sentiments. Even authors who demonstrate the negative effects of religion on African societies admit that religion is pertinent to social change in Africa.

Second, the empirical data and literature underscore the need for widows' agency. The widows believe they can effect social change, although they seemed overwhelmed about the prospect of contributing to social change because widowhood has become a tool for oppression. As I observed them shopping, cooking, socializing, and learning, it was clear that their experiences as widows have only served to inhibit them from seeing their roles as agents of social change. Most of the literature does not address the agency of widows; rather, the literature focuses on the issues of remarriage and property inheritance, which undermine the widows' agency. Moreover, feminist literatures that underscore women's agency do not speak glowingly of the women's roles as "wives" and "mothers." But the widows considered these roles essential to their agency. Therefore, I picked up my conversation on agency by addressing the widows' existing roles and how those roles position them for greater achievements within society.

Third, the literature and empirical data note the role of institutions in guiding the widows' agency. The widows acknowledged that government institutions have failed to help them access the resources needed to enhance their lives. For this research, I also visited the churches where most of the widows attended. I spoke with the people in those churches about their perception of the widows. The pastors and elders, for instance, raved about the widows and the roles the widows play to enhance communal worship. The widows were resolute that only Christian institutions can best guide their agency. I also interviewed a couple of Muslim widows and widows who converted from Islam to Christianity. Their responses support the claims of Christian widows that Christian institutions best guide widows' agency. I should add that both Christian and Muslim widows provided both pushback and endorsement of the literature as it pertains to how Christian institutions help widows. Although there are some disagreements on the effectiveness of Christian institutions to guide the agency of widows, the empirical research and literature agree that Christian institutions best guide widows' agency.

Fourth, the widows desire to know their potential to effect social change. Embodiment became evident in our conversations. In discussions about deaths, one envisions the dead body of husbands, the bodies of their children, and even the bodies of prostitutes and other women their husbands slept with. But it is the widows' bodies I focus on here. First, the widows talk about their bodies in relation to how they were maltreated and objectified by society. But second, I also observed the ways that the widows use their bodies in relation to the world around them. During my interviews, for instance, I noticed how the widows' gestures made their stories more compelling. Those non-verbal cues contributed immensely to my understanding of the plight of widows in northern Nigeria. For instance, some widows shook their heads as they narrated their stories. In northern Nigeria, a widow who shakes her head while telling her story is her way of telling you, "I can't even begin to make you fully understand the gravity of what I've been through." This feeds off into the position that feminist theologians make in their analyses of womanhood in Africa. While most of the feminist literature tends to treat the issues of African women uniformly, some of the literature recognizes the diverse experiences of African women. Embodiment demands we recognize the diverse experiences of widows to position them to best determine what widows could potentially do with agency.

In sum, I noted that widows have no power to effect change. Since this study stems from a Christian theology, I focused on the interactions between the literature and the empirical data that address the ways

Christianity empowers widows towards agency. In his article "Rethinking Power in Africa," Elias K. Bongmba reflects on theological viewpoints on power.[22] He argues that the aim of power is to engender greater freedom of people in society.[23] According to Bongmba, power is an appropriate subject to bring up because of the culture of suffering within Africa. Bongmba argues that reconstructing a way to adequately address socio-economic and political crises requires addressing the issue of power and whether religion can be a tool towards a brighter future for Africa.

Bongmba's argument rises out of the voices of some African theologians who champion what Charles Villa-Vicencio describes as "a theology of reconstruction."[24] This theology undertakes the search for human rights in a new context. Feminist theologies embrace this reconstructionist theology of Bongmba in two ways. First, although feminist theology rises from the liberation theology of the 1960s, it aims to move beyond just liberation to reconstruction.[25] And, second, as reconstructionist theology, feminist theologians establish the fact that creation has a purpose for existence. Beverly Harrison, a feminist theologian, refers to power as "the ability to act on and effectually shape the world around us."[26] Therefore, I examine how widows' social status positions them to use power in transformative ways within society.

Delimitations of the Study

This study contributes to Africa's quest for social change. However, there are delimitations to the study. First, I focus on Nigeria, specifically on northern Nigeria. Second, I highlight the works that engage the topic of women's role towards societal change. These works also reflect the integration between the church and the culture. Third, I consider widows, not all women in northern Nigeria. I acknowledge that there are women of varying statuses in northern Nigeria. Next, I focus specifically on Christian widows in northern Nigeria, and not all widows. While the experiences of Christian widows and other widows might have similarities, it is the experiences of

---

22. Bongmba, "Rethinking Power," 103–38.

23. Bongmba, "Rethinking Power," 103.

24. Villa-Vicencio, *A Theology of Reconstruction*. See also Getui and Obeng, *Theology of Reconstruction*.

25. Mugambi, *From Liberation to Reconstruction*.

26. Harrison, *Making the Connection*, 250.

Methodological Issues

Christian widows I present in this study. Also, it is important to note that this study focuses on the widows and not their children, although both groups are closely linked since conversations with the widows resulted in discussions about their children.

Significance of the Study

The purpose of this study is to understand the role of Christian widows in northern Nigeria, who represent a community of saints practicing their faith in a predominantly Islamic region of the country. Thus, this study contributes to the documentation and systematic study of Christian religious expression in an Islamic-dominant region in the context of world Christianity. This will be one of only a few thorough accounts of the role of widows in northern Nigeria.

The study contributes to the literature on the phenomena of widowhood across the globe. For too long, detailed study of widowhood has either been ignored or rejected because it is considered "taboo." My ethnographic approach describes two organizations that seek to empower widows towards agency. I provide a description that would help in further research to evaluate ongoing attempts at empowering widows and develop creative approaches of widow empowerment that engender widows' agency.

I underscore the importance of the role of laity such as widows in the society, paying attention to the roles widows play in northern Nigeria over the years. Their stories stress the need for community development, especially in a largely poor northern Nigeria. Moreover, this study provides a portrayal of societal changes influenced by the dedication of widows.

The point is that widows are fulfilling the mission of God in an Islamic context that is characterized by marginality and persecution. Therefore, they demonstrate Christian mission in a courageous way.

1. This study provides an understanding of the church's holistic vision in northern Nigeria.
2. This study analyzes the role of widows in northern Nigeria, and its implication to the transformation of northern Nigeria.

2

Religion and Agency

ZAINAB WAS THE OLDEST widow I interviewed at about seventy years of age. The wrinkles on her face alone tell Zainab's heartwrenching tale. Like most women in northern Nigeria, she married when she was only a teenager because it was the "right thing" to do.[1] When they got married, her husband was an ambitious young man in his late twenties. His ambition was to join the Nigerian army and rise the ranks to provide for his family. As Christians, they prayed for this dream to come to reality. Several years and five children later, her husband finally joined the army. But rising to the ranks required many sacrifices of his young family. He was gone for weeks and months for military service, leaving his young wife and five children. The army paid enough for them to live a comfortable life, but his absence placed a lot of pressure on Zainab. Things got worse when her husband never returned home after one of his military assignments.

Several months, after much inquiry, he was officially declared missing, although Zainab knew he was dead. The army stopped providing any financial assistance to her. Her in-laws confiscated all her property, expelling her and her children from the house. With five children to care for, Zainab had no choice but return to her husband's village. She received no sympathy from her in-laws; in fact, they accused her of killing her husband. What was worse, they blamed her children for colluding with their mother to kill their father. To prove her innocence, she agreed to undergo the mourning

1. In Zainab's village, people believe that early marriage prevents promiscuity.

widowhood rituals required of widows in northern Nigeria. But that did not satisfy her in-laws. She watched as her in-laws branded her children with hot iron to ensure they were not responsible for their father's disappearance.

However, at seventy years, Zainab tells her story with a deep sense of gratitude to God. "I thank God for everything. It was God that allowed everything to happen, and I cannot argue with God."[2] Zainab says this despite all she has been through. She was emphatic that her faith in God has continued to sustain her. In short, Zainab's embodiment is part of her religious expression, a correlation I demonstrate in this study. As I already noted, her submission to God gave her hope for a brighter future. And this faith undergirds her widowhood experiences, particularly the mourning rituals in which widows like her participate. In fact, because religion undergirds widows' lives in northern Nigeria, all my respondents see widowhood as a divine charge towards agency.

In this chapter, I argue that religion undergirds the agency of Christian widows in northern Nigeria. I establish the important correlation between religion and widows' agency in northern Nigeria by demonstrating that northern Nigeria's history consists of religious antecedents that influence the lives of Christian widows throughout their lives, especially from their marital homes to their widowhood. This leads into conversation about how the interaction between religion and social change represents the combination of local rituals and Christian rites. I conclude by demonstrating the important role Christianity plays towards the widows' agency.

The Context of Christian Widows in Northern Nigeria

In *The Sacrifice of Africa*, Emmanuel Katongole demonstrates that modern Africa is disfigured by its established narratives of colonial repression and nation-state politics.[3] Therefore, modern Africa has remained susceptible to chaos, war, and corruption. In short, Katongole states that Africa is caught in an endless cycle of violence, plunder, and poverty as Africa's human and material resources have been exploited and sacrificed to the greedy ambitions of oppressive governments.[4] Katongole suggests that this is a narrative Africans inhabit post colonialism. Katongole challenges this distressing legacy and reveals that this narrative continues to distort the

2. Zainab, interview by author, April 23, 2017.
3. Katongole, *Sacrifice of Africa*.
4. Katongole, *Sacrifice of Africa*, 1.

creative potential of African politics and society. Katongole demonstrates Christianity's potential to interject to change rooted political creativity and build a different African narrative. One of the areas where Africa's painful legacy is evident is in the plight of widows across the continent.

The story of Zainab reveals the deep despair that many widows in northern Nigeria face. Zainab's story is a compelling account of the influence religion has on women in northern Nigeria. Religious sentiments undergird her despair (i.e., mourning rituals), yet it is the same religious sentiments that seem to sustain Zainab's hopes for a brighter future. To buttress his point, Katongole also presents compelling stories to illustrate how African people are resisting the narrative of death and embracing a new narrative of hope for the continent.[5] But Katongole underscores the role that Christianity must play in interrupting Africa's warped imaginations while creating a better future for Africa. In short, Katongole recognizes that religion plays a decisive role in the imaginations and narratives of Africans. Thus, we cannot understand the context of widows in northern Nigeria without comprehending how religion shapes their experiences. But before delving into the discussion on how religion undergirds the lives of widows such as Zainab in northern Nigeria, it is important to locate northern Nigeria.

Locating northern Nigeria is important for three reasons. (1) Obviously, northern Nigeria is where the widows I researched live. To understand their experiences necessitates knowledge of the history of the land they occupy. (2) Understanding the history of northern Nigeria would include understanding the religious history that shapes the experiences of widows. (3) Coming to terms with this religious history is pertinent towards engendering widows' embodied agency in northern Nigeria.

Locating Northern Nigeria

The land that is now called "Nigeria" was known for the Nok culture (1500 BC–500 AD), which provided terracotta figures considered among the earliest recognized sculptures in Africa.[6] In the medieval ages (1500–1800 BC), Nigeria began to see territorial expansions because existing monarchies in western and northern Nigeria began to assert their dominance both within and outside Nigeria.[7] In northern Nigeria, the effective "jihad"

---

5. Katongole, *Sacrifice of Africa*, 135–92.
6. Rupp, Breunig and Kahlheber, "Exploring the Nok Enigma."
7. Metz, "Nigeria."

spearheaded by Usman dan Fodio meant he controlled much of northern and central Nigeria until the British came and disbanded the territories into several colonies.

British Influence

The British influenced what became northern Nigeria. In the nineteenth century, most of the area now called Nigeria was ruled by the Royal Niger Company (RNC). The RNC was a chartered company under the administration of Sir George Taubman Goldie, who played a decisive role in the consolidation of Nigeria. This is because during Goldie's tenure, the Southern and Northern Protectorates of Nigeria moved from the control of the RNC to the monarchy. Frederick Lugard, the governor of what became Nigeria, urged that the two Protectorates be merged. In 1914, the amalgamation happened as the beginnings of the new nation called "Nigeria."

However, post-World War II, the global reformists staunchly advocated for increased representation and electoral government by the Nigerian people, which resulted in Nigeria's independence in 1960. Nevertheless, independence would be the beginning of great challenges for Nigeria. The major reason for these challenges is religion. Thus, by amalgamating the predominantly Muslim north and largely Christian south in 1914, the colonialists initiated the perpetual ethno-religious violence in northern Nigeria. In the colonialists' drive towards control, the colonialists failed to consider the implications of merging two regions with significantly complex ideologies that shape their diverse and unique cultural practices.

Nigeria

Today, Nigeria is a federal republic in West Africa. It borders Benin to the west, Chad and Cameroon to the east, and Niger to the north. Its southern coastline lies on the Gulf of Guinea in the Atlantic Ocean. Nigeria consists of thirty-six states and the Federal Capital Territory (FCT) in Abuja. Nigeria is officially recognized as a secular state.[8] Due to its large population of approximately 200 million people, and a potentially vibrant economy,[9] Nigeria is considered the "Giant of Africa."[10] It is considered a multinational

---

8. Federal Republic of Nigeria, "Constitution."
9. The Guardian, "Nigeria Becomes Africa's Largest Economy."
10. Holmes, *Nigeria*.

state, since it consists of over 250 ethnic groups that speak over 500 different languages.[11] However, the three largest ethnic groups are Hausa, Yoruba, and Igbo. Nigeria is still divided between Christians, who live mostly in the southern part of the country, and Muslims, who are the majority in the north. The concern of this study is northern Nigeria.

Northern Nigeria

As noted above, northern Nigerian history accounts for the history of the region from pre-historic to modern times. The Nok culture was an ancient culture that dominated most parts of northern Nigeria in prehistoric periods. Its heritage of terracotta statues and megaliths have been found in various parts of northern Nigeria (i.e., Sokoto, Kano, Kaduna, and Zaria). Between circa 500 AD and 700 AD, the Hausa-Muslim people gradually moved from Nubia and integrated with the local northern and Middle Belt populations, creating several vibrant states in what has become northern Nigeria and eastern Niger. When Nok and Sokoto diminished, after controlling central and northern Nigeria between 800 BC and 200 AD, the Hausa people emerged as the new power in the region. The Hausa-Muslim aristocracy, influenced by the Mali Empire, embraced Islam in the eleventh century AD. In the twelfth century AD, the Hausa-Muslims emerged as one of Africa's major powers.

One of the fascinating things about Hausa-Muslims of northern Nigeria was their architecture. Architecture became a major religious expression for the Hausa-Muslims. They have produced some of the best architecture of the medieval age. Many early mosques and palaces were bright and brilliant, and included delicate symbols designed into the edifice. In northern Nigeria today, the Hausa-Muslims replicate such designs in the building of mosques. But the buildings stand in contrast to the people of northern Nigeria, who are considered among the poorest in the country. Women, including widows, make up the largest population of the poor in northern Nigeria. Poverty does not only affect Muslim widows, but it is a major factor in the lives of Christian widows in northern Nigeria.

11. Otite, "Nigeria's Identifiable Ethnic Groups."

Poverty and Widowhood in Northern Nigeria

Nigeria is one of Africa's largest economies, with an estimated gross domestic product (GDP) at $480 billion.[12] However, despite economic diversification and resilient growth, poverty levels, particularly among women, remain high, at 70 percent. People in northern Nigeria are extremely poor. Of the six geopolitical zones in Nigeria, there are three in northern Nigeria (Northwest, North-central, and Northeast). According to Aslam Khan and Lawan Cheri, these three parts of northern Nigeria contain the worst indices of poverty in the country.[13] Widows in northern Nigeria are particularly impacted by the unpredictability of a complex, mutating, and attenuated economic environment that is subject to natural and man-made forces.[14] Consequently, Nigerian widows are poor in more than one facet of life. Poverty affects Christian widows in northern Nigeria. They lack basic human needs such as shelter, clothing, and food. In other words, they do not have access to resources that can enable them to overcome deprivation, which renders them powerless to effect any social change.

Pat Okoye states that poverty is the factor that influences punitive widowhood practices in Nigeria.[15] Okoye suggests that poverty exposes the widow to people's evil schemes.[16] What Okoye's point demonstrates is that poverty sanctions the maltreatment of widows. Okoye also makes an important point when he says that it is not only the poverty of the widow that puts her at risk of maltreatment, but also the poverty of her in-laws and society that promote the scramble for the widow's property. In short, the widow does not only suffer due to her own poverty but the poverty of those who exploit her.

But what gives potency to widows' economic deprivations is the overarching religious sentiment that operates within northern Nigeria. Religion is behind the factors that lead to the socio-economic challenges of Christian widows in northern Nigeria. Unfortunately, most social scientists attribute the causes of poverty in northern Nigeria to mismanagement of resources, failed policies, and corruption.[17] These are certainly valid causes; however,

---

12. CIA, "Nigeria."
13. Khan and Cheri, "Examination of Poverty," 59–71.
14. Buvinic, Lycette, and McGreevey, *Women and Poverty in the Third World*, 152.
15. Okoye, *Widowhood*, 226.
16. Okoye, *Widowhood*, 226.
17. Ngbea and Achunike, "Poverty in Northern Nigeria."

most social scientists neglect the fact that the major cause of extreme poverty in northern Nigeria is *religion*. Khan and Cheri reveal a strong religious correlation to poverty in the region.[18] The authors show the link between the persistent religious crises in northern Nigeria and the poverty indicators that initiated the ongoing turmoil. They argue that poverty is the seed that produced the Islamic sect known as *Boko Haram*.[19] This radical sect, whose name means "Western influence is bad," has wreaked havoc in the region for close to twenty years.[20] But poverty did not only produce Boko Haram; Boko Haram has also exacerbated the poverty that pervades northern Nigeria. Moreover, ethno-religious violence that amplifies the poverty of widows in northern Nigeria also leads to their marginalization and thus undermines widows' agency.

Because of the religious correlations to their poverty, the widows expressed great faith in God's power to overcome their challenges. In fact, when they bemoan their inability to provide for their children due to very little to no resources, they conclude with the assurance that God can meet their needs. Therefore, religion does not produce their poverty; poverty drives their religious zeal. They recognize that a strong faith in God is the remedy to overcoming their challenges and become agents of social change. To understand why faith is important for widows in northern Nigeria, we need to further explore the religious topography of northern Nigeria. This is important in determining that religious antecedent influences how widows exercise their agency in northern Nigeria.

Religion in Northern Nigeria

Okoye states that every principle, prescription, and sanction that influences human behavior in Nigeria is derived from religion.[21] In northern Nigeria, religion is the greatest social force because even people in secular positions consider religion pertinent to carrying out their responsibilities. Religion in northern Nigeria is not confined to shrines, temples, or buildings; it is congruent to an African sense of their humanity.

18. Khan and Cheri, "Examination of Poverty," 65.
19. Khan and Cheri, "Examination of Poverty," 66.
20. For more details on Boko Haram, see Thurston, *Boko Haram*. Thurston argues that Boko Haram represents the outcome of dynamic and locally grounded interactions between religion and politics.
21. Okoye, *Widowhood*, 135.

In northern Nigeria, there are three major religions: *African traditional religions (ATR), Islam, and Christianity.* These religions are strong cultural forces and are key components of people's social consciousness. There are also overlaps between the three religions. As the oldest religious expression in northern Nigeria, African traditional religion (ATR) exerts significant influence on Islam and Christianity.[22] ATR's influence on ethnic groups in northern Nigeria that identify as Christian or Muslim makes the study of religion in Africa challenging.[23] It certainly makes Zainab's story challenging because her innocence was complicated by cultural demands. And this "weaving" of her Christian faith and culture is characteristic of African cosmology, which refers to the way that Africans understand and reflect upon the universe.[24] Africans' vision of reality influences the value systems and behaviors that help them in their search for meaning. African cosmology is foundational to the values, philosophies, myths, rituals, rites, concepts, and theologies that shape Africans of every religion.

African Cosmology

Okoye notes that a person's behavior is influenced by his worldview.[25] Thus, people's traditions and customs stem from their cosmology. The African worldview is made up of many systems, beliefs, and perceptions that crystallized over time as people interacted with the environment. The African worldview deals with matters of reality, value, and meanings that Africans place in creation, which are handed down through the generations. Some of the key aspects of African cosmology include the existence of God, physical/spiritual dimensions, divine agents, and humanity. Below, I briefly describe these important aspects of African cosmology that are specific to northern Nigeria, since there are wide differences on these key aspects across Africa.

---

22. Oduyoye, *Daughters of Anowa*, 12.

23. The expression "African traditional religions" suggests the strong link between religion and culture in Africa. Therefore, to speak of religion in this study is to equally speak of culture. I will be using the terms "religion" and "culture" interchangeably here; however, I will distinguish them when necessary to indicate their specific influence within the African worldview.

24. Kanu, "The Dimensions of African Cosmology," 533.

25. Okoye, *Widowhood*, 129.

First, God is an important reality in African cosmology.[26] Africans believe that God is personable and approachable.[27] God, who is male, is regarded as the king who looks out for the best interests of his people. He goes by several names, with each name depicting the theme individual African groups consider preeminent in their interaction with God. But God has some unifying attributes that concern his activity in the world, his uniqueness, his absolute power over creation, his oneness, his creative prowess, his kingship, his omnipotence, and his eternality.[28]

Second, there are physical and spiritual dimensions within African cosmology.[29] In the spiritual realm, God has the ultimate power over all creation. In the physical realm, man occupies and exercises his God-given powers. The physical world consists of the sky, earth, and underworld. Thus, the physical and spiritual dimensions interact because God has power over everything.

Third, Africans believe that God has intermediaries. These intermediaries come from God but are not created by God. Rather, they are children of God. These intermediaries attend to trivial issues that arise within creation, although God must approve everything they do.[30] These divine agents are referred to as "spirits" and "ancestors." There are many spirits within African cosmology. Africans believe that upon death people's souls return to God. Therefore, since humans interact with God, Africans also see themselves as perpetually interacting with the living dead. The "living death" also refers to the supernatural status of an African ancestor who is considered a moral exemplar.

Finally, African cosmology is anthropocentric.[31] In other words, Africans consider everything as made for man. In fact, John Mbiti states that "it is as if God exists for the sake of man."[32] Thus, "God, divinities, ancestors, rituals, and sacrifices are only useful to the extent that they serve the need of man."[33] However, man's existence depends on God. Consequently, man has a purpose to fulfill on earth. Wealth, health, and prosperity are indicative

26. Quarcoopome, *West African Traditional Religion*.
27. Idowu, *Oludumare: God in Yoruba Belief*.
28. Kanu, "The Dimensions of African Cosmology," 537–39.
29. Ijiomah, "African Philosophy's Contributions," 81–90.
30. Awolalu and Dopamu, *West African Traditional Religion*.
31. Mbiti, *African Religions and Philosophy*.
32. Mbiti, *African Religions and Philosophy*, 92.
33. Kanu, "The Dimensions of African Cosmology," 550.

of one's good standing with God. Therefore, we can only comprehend man by his appropriate relationship with God.

There are some variances of these fundamental aspects of African cosmology within Christianity that would be evident in this study. And this is because these fundamental aspects of African cosmology have been handed down through the generations, including today's widowhood practices.[34] Thus, widowhood practices such as mourning rituals within African cultures are rooted in cosmological insights.[35] As a result, it is safe to assert that religious antecedents shape the lives of African women.[36]

One of the major areas where African cosmology finds expression is within African marriages. Given the religious underpinning of marriage, it is no wonder that feminist theologians claim that describing African women's experiences must begin by studying the African woman within marriage. Feminist theologians conclude that a woman does not have any power in traditional marriage in Africa.[37] Marriage is considered the transfer of the woman from one suzerain (father) to another (husband).[38] In other words, marriage perpetuated Zainab's powerlessness and marginality. The implementation of marriage laws within northern Nigeria demonstrates the powerlessness and marginalization of women in northern Nigeria. A discussion on the types of marriages in northern Nigeria reveals this powerlessness and marginalization that persists into widowhood. Most importantly, the powerlessness and marginalization revealed in the types of marriages demonstrates that religion undergirds the marriage realities of African women.

Types of Marriages in Northern Nigeria

The Marriage Act of Nigeria recognizes the voluntary union of one man and one woman.[39] However, the Marriage Act places types of marriages in Nigeria under two categories: *statutory* and *customary*. Statutory refers to Nigeria's secular law that endorses marriage as monogamous. But statutory marriages are influenced by the religious peculiarities of those who compose

34. Okoye, *Widowhood*, 132.
35. Iheanacho, "The Alienation of Nigerian Women in Widowhood," 21.
36. Oduyoye, *Daughters of Anowa*, 21.
37. Oduyoye, *Daughters of Anowa*, 134–35.
38. Oduyoye, *Daughters of Anowa*, 135.
39. Federal Republic of Nigeria, "Marriage Act, chapter 218."

them. As I noted, religion's social force is so strong that even secular aspects of lives in northern Nigeria have religious underpinnings. Customary marriage laws, on the other hand, are founded upon religious tenets. While some customary marriages are monogamous, they tend to be more polygamous. Customary marriage laws greatly influence Christian widows in northern Nigeria. While Christian marriage laws endorse monogamy, churches permit polygamy in the unique circumstances I discuss below.

Thus, the two categories of marriage produced two major types of marriages in northern Nigeria: *monogamous* and *polygamous* marriages. Monogamous marriage is the marriage of one person at a time. Polygamous marriage is the marriage of multiple spouses at a time. There are also two types of polygamous marriages: "polyandry," the marriage of one woman to multiple men at a time, and "polygyny," the marriage of one man to multiple women at a time.[40]

Polygamy continues to be practiced in northern Nigeria even by Christians. Churches baptize members in polygamous marriages.[41] Thus, churches do not insist on separating or divorcing one's multiple partners after becoming Christians. The churches' decision has far-reaching impacts for widows. While I did not interview widows who were directly involved in polygamous marriages that churches permitted, several widows I interviewed talked about the effects of polygamy on them although they were in monogamous marriages. Because they felt Christianity legitimized polygamy, they readily accepted it.

Upon her husband's death, Hauwa narrated how she found out her husband had fathered several children from several women while they were married. She invited the other wives and their children to her home to

---

40. While polygyny is common across most tribes in northern Nigeria, polyandry is very rare. The Irigwe people of northern Nigeria are one of two African tribes that practice a form of polyandry. Polyandry among the Irigwe takes the shape of secondary marriages. This has to do with a woman who marries "secondary husbands" while married to her primary husband. Such an arrangement enables her to preserve her prerogative to have children with any of her husbands. When Walter H. Sangree conducted his ethnographic research on the Irigwe people, polyandry had just been enacted (Sangree, "The Persistence of Polyandry in Irigwe, Nigeria," 335–43). Unfortunately, there is no current research to determine if the practice still exists among the Irigwe (See Starkweather, "A Preliminary Survey of Lesser-Known Polyandrous Societies," 25; Levine and Sangree, "Conclusion," 385–410).

41. I should note that the only "acceptable" polygamous unions churches accept are of men who had multiple wives before becoming Christians or those participating in levirate unions.

formally meet them. When asked what motivated her to reach out to them, she replied, "What do you expect me to do? I had to do what was morally right."[42] What I found out was that it was her pastor who counseled her to reach out to them. Thus, even if Hauwa had other ways she wanted to respond to her husband's mistresses and their children, she became bound by her pastor's counsel. She believed her pastor knew what was right for her even if she disagreed. She said the pastor referenced several biblical texts to convince her to set aside her needs for the sake of others. Unfortunately, she could not remember those biblical texts at the time of our interview. However, African cosmology provides some explanation for her decision to embrace her dead husband's estranged wives and children. In African cosmology, the implication that God exists for men's sake is that women also exist for men's sake. "Submission" is a word African women are very familiar with: submission to their fathers, husbands, and pastors are normative. African women regard these men as their "spiritual mentors" whose words must be adhered to. These and other religious sentiments within marriage laws in northern Nigeria perpetuate a sense of powerlessness and marginalization of African women.

Marriage, Widowhood, and Powerlessness in Northern Nigeria

The contention of feminist theologians is that the religious antecedents that undergird marriage in Africa promote a low view of women. Patrilineality is one of such social systems in northern Nigeria with religious antecedents. Patrilineality is behind the patriarchy feminist theologians vehemently oppose; in fact, the patriarchal society of northern Nigeria is also patrilineal. Patrilineality is a system where people are accounted kin through the male, or agnatic, line.[43] Although fraternity can also be created through matrilineal or ideological ties, patrilineality is the most precise and robust medium of attaining the fraternal alliance required to provide group security.[44] Patrilineality is meant to create a fraternal alliance system of brothers, cousins, sons, uncles, and fathers capable of countering threats to the group. In short, patrilineality aims to provide physical and economic security for male kin in northern Nigeria.

---

42. Hauwa, interview by author, March 27, 2017.
43. Stone, *Kinship and Gender*.
44. Hudson and Matfess, "In Plain Sight," 12.

Women, on the other hand, lack both physical and economic security. Men are given property rights or "marital rights on women."[45] Therefore, women move between kinship groups in exogamous marriage and thus, in a sense, are not full kin in patrilineal societies.[46] In patrilineal society, the norms of tenure favor men because men are considered custodians of land.[47] Marriage in patrilineal societies is accompanied by asset exchange, where bride price offsets the cost to the natal family for raising the bride.

In examining the linkages between socioeconomic characteristics, attitudes, and familial contraceptive use, Mustapha C. Duze and Ismaila Z. Mohammed show that family planning programs have been largely directed towards women. Their conclusion is that northern Nigeria (and to an extent all of Nigeria) remains a patrilineal society since men determine familial fertility and contraceptive decisions.[48] What this suggests is that men are not only responsible for male ritual roles such as farming, hunting, and harvesting; men also control female roles. For instance, Walter H. Sangree demonstrates that the Irigwe people of northern Nigeria divide what are called male and female halves.[49] However, in this patrilinear society, men perform both "male" and "female" roles. Men carry out ritual designated for males, i.e., storing, bush firing, hunting, and the beginning of sowing. But, men also carry out rituals designated for females, i.e., farming and harvesting. In fact, "rituals for fertility, for which women would naturally seem more competent, were carried out by men taking on the role of women."[50] The consequences that grow out of this system are detrimental to the security and status of women in northern Nigeria.[51]

Rather than gain value, most women in northern Nigeria have diminished value within their matrimonial homes. A diminished value at home results in diminished value within society at large, where women lack power to effect significant changes.[52] Even if one contends that women have

---

45. Hudson and Matfess, "In Plain Sight," 12.
46. Hudson and Matfess, "In Plain Sight," 12.
47. Duncan, "Cocoa, Marriage, Labour and Land in Ghana," 302.
48. Duze and Mohammed, "Male Knowledge, Attitudes, and Family Planning," 53–65.
49. Sangree, "Tribal Ritual, Leadership and the Mortality Rate in Irigwe," 32–39.
50. Sangree, "Tribal Ritual, Leadership and the Mortality Rate in Irigwe," 33; see also Frank, "Gendered Ritual Dualism," 217–40.
51. Hudson and Matfess, "In Plain Sight," 12.
52. Bonat, "Challenges of Widowhood."

power, the power is very limited. Hassana, a middle-aged widow, spoke about how marriage subjects many women to a life of great struggle. And the struggles intensify when the woman's husband dies. In fact, if women have any power, the power disappears when they become widows. In other words, the detrimental consequences of patrilinealism become more evident when a northern Nigerian woman becomes a widow.

Hassana expressed dismay at the ways widows are viewed in northern Nigeria: "Where we come from, widows are considered of no value."[53] As Hassana notes, widows face even greater challenges because they lack any power to effect change. Therefore, religious sentiments continue to undergird women's lives into their widowhood. Particularly, religion promotes the mourning rituals that widows undergo. And the mourning rituals are closely linked to the perception of the causes of deaths. This link represents the lived realities of Christian widows in northern Nigeria that disempower them. What strengthens this link are strong religious sentiments that undergird both mourning rituals and the causes of deaths. I demonstrate this link by describing the causes of deaths and mourning rituals.

Causes of Death: Accidents and Conflicts

A not-for-profit group conducted ethnographic research to determine the community's needs in a northern Nigerian village; they discovered that Ambam, a village of 1200 people, had over one hundred widows.[54] Their findings showed that the widows' husbands died due to accidents, snakebites, sickness, HIV/AIDS, unknown causes, spiritual attacks, and religious violence.[55] Other than one widow who told me that she found out later her husband died of HIV/AIDS, most of the widows informed me that their husbands died of two broad reasons: *accidents* and *conflicts*. For these widows, accidents and conflicts are caused by sicknesses and the incessant ethno-religious violence in northern Nigeria. What these two major categories demonstrate is that religion undergirds the reasons for the deaths of widows' husbands in northern Nigeria.

---

53. Hassana, interview by author, March 16, 2017.
54. Bauta, "Empowering Widows," 10.
55. Madinger, *Widows of Ambam Kaninkon*.

Accidents

Accidents occur especially on the farm, although they can occur anywhere. When a woman's husband is bitten by a poisonous snake, for instance, the family is thrown into chaos. There is the need to take care of the health emergency, but finances are very limited. Therefore, accidents become a major strain on the family, financially and emotionally. When Grace's husband became sick, she bore the brunt of the financial and emotional burden.[56] She spent time and money to nurse her husband back to health. By the time the husband died (or even if he had survived), she was faced with a depleted bank account, debts, and alienation. But if she does not care for him, she would be accused of killing him through witchcraft.[57] This underscores the fact that most people attribute accidents to spiritual attacks in northern Nigeria. Accidents represent the perpetual conflict of good and evil over people, and women make up a majority of its casualties because the consequences of every religious conflict are visited upon the widows.

Conflicts

The history of violent conflicts in northern Nigeria goes as far back as the 1950s. Religion is the primary reason for the conflict because even economic and political conflicts have religious angles. These conflicts have resulted in the deaths of many of the widows' husbands. Despite several decades of conflicts in the region, perhaps the most defining has been the Boko Haram situation.[58] Boko Haram is responsible for the deaths of approximately 100,000 people and has destroyed properties worth billions of dollars.

As already noted, religion undergirds Boko Haram's activities. And this is not to suggest that cultural change and marginalization in terms of economics, for instance, are not significant factors. However, religion enhances the cultural change and marginalization based on economics. Most of the husbands of the Christian widows died due to the ethno-religious conflicts initiated by Boko Haram. Hassana's husband was murdered during Boko Haram's attacks on her village.[59] She narrates how, sensing danger approaching, her husband sent her and her children to a safe zone while he

---

56. Grace, interview by author, April 2, 2017.
57. Oduyoye, *Daughters of Anowa*, 30–31.
58. BBC, "Who Are Nigeria's Boko Haram Islamists?"
59. Hassana, interview by author, March 16, 2017.

remained with the other men to defend their village against Boko Haram. Unfortunately, Hassana and her children returned after the violence to discover his scorched body on the steps of their burnt house.

Hassana largely sees her husband's death as a "spiritual attack." In fact, what connects accidents and conflicts is the issue of witchcraft. The three neighboring countries of Chad, Cameroon, and Nigeria have all endured the mayhem perpetuated by Boko Haram. These countries utilized guns and bombs to repel the sect, but they have proven to be ineffective. Consequently, witchcraft is being utilized by some of these countries as a strategy against Boko Haram.[60] This is enforced by the fact that religion is the primary motivator for Boko Haram. It is fascinating, however, that African governments are willing to use witchcraft, an "illegal" technique, to consolidate their power; but widows are accused and demonized for allegedly using witchcraft to improve their lived realities. More needs to be said about witchcraft because it underscores the religious antecedent of widows' lived realities in northern Nigeria.

On Witchcraft

Because every cause of death has a religious angle to it, widows consider the causes of their husbands' deaths as spiritual attacks. Paul C. Rosenblatt and Busisiwe C. Nkosi note that African widows struggle with the issue of witchcraft either as the cause of deaths or accusation directed at the widows.[61] What the authors mean is that witchcraft is tied to every cause of death. And because witchcraft is seen as the territory of women,[62] widows are the primary suspects when their husbands die. Mercy Oduyoye notes that African societies expect women to use "mystical powers to avenge themselves" against male oppression.[63] In fact, African societies even consider the silence of women as "witchcraft." In other words, the silence of women is perceived as part of a plot to aggressively attack men. Oduyoye attributes this thinking about women's plots to attack men to the myths emanating from African cosmology, which views women as more brutal than men when given access to power.[64] This is enhanced by the depictions of

---

60. Locka, "Cameroon Uses Witchcraft to Fight Boko Haram."
61. Rosenblatt and Nkosi, "South African Zulu Widows," 74.
62. Oduyoye, *Daughters of Anowa*, 40–41.
63. Oduyoye, *Daughters of Anowa*, 30.
64. Oduyoye, *Daughters of Anowa*, 40.

old women as witches in African folktales.⁶⁵ Being a widow only enhances the belief about the supposed evil proclivities of African women. By that, I am referring to Oduyoye's suggestion that widows are seen as women who chose to kill their husbands via witchcraft rather than continue to allow society to shape their lives.⁶⁶ In other words, widows are believed to use witchcraft to overcome patriarchal suppression at home.

The issue of witchcraft has to do with power. Feminist theologians such as Oduyoye are convinced that African societies are intimidated by powerful women; thus, society does everything possible to deny women power. Therefore, feminist theologians critique the religious sentiments that suggest widows must undergo mourning rituals to prove they are innocent of their husbands' deaths. There is credence to such critique because those beliefs are based on speculations that are subject to cultural interpretations. Therefore, this study focuses on the religious sentiment that mourning rituals are a "rite of passage" for widows. In other words, widowhood is a ceremony towards agency. Particularly, widowhood is a state where widows consider how to exercise their agency.

My point is that witchcraft demonstrates that religion engenders the link between the causes of the deaths of widows' husbands and the mourning rituals. Describing the mourning rituals in northern Nigeria is essential to this study because rituals are central arenas towards social change. Therefore, I describe the mourning rituals that widows in northern Nigeria undergo upon the deaths of their husbands. I demonstrate that the mourning rituals are fundamentally based on the assertion that widowhood is a "rite of passage." The issue of rite of passage becomes pertinent to the role Christianity plays in the agency of Christian widows in northern Nigeria.

Coming to Terms with Mourning Rituals in Northern Nigeria

The rationale behind widowhood practices is that widowhood is a transitory state that requires the widow to enter via rituals of separation and emerge through rites of reincorporation.⁶⁷ The aim of the rituals is to ensure the integrated life of the widow even if that includes pain, exploitation, and deprivation. Widowhood practices assume that dead husbands

65. Oduyoye, *Daughters of Anowa*, 40.
66. Oduyoye, *Daughters of Anowa*, 30.
67. Iheanacho, "Alienation of Nigerian Women," 21.

continue to exist on earth as spirits, acquiring more powers for evil towards the widows. Widows in northern Nigeria are believed to be dragged by the living and the dead at the early phase of mourning.[68] This thinking follows the idea that widows might have killed their husbands through witchcraft, a position I suggest is based on subjective interpretations of societal laws.

However, the notion that their dead husbands would harm them enforces rituals that are believed to liberate widows from the actions of the spirit-world.[69] Therefore, religion undergirds the mourning rituals widows undergo in northern Nigeria. Pat Okoye demonstrates that religion plays a decisive role in determining widowhood practices.[70] Ngozi Iheanacho also notes that Africans view "the practices of widowhood through the prism of religious conviction and phenomenon."[71] The mourning ritual is the major feature in widowhood practices in northern Nigeria. Dan Alumka specifically states that mourning rituals are primarily enforced by religious sentiments in northern Nigeria.[72]

The Mourning Ritual in Northern Nigeria

Before she considers remarriage or other ventures, an African widow must complete the mourning ritual. Widows commence what is called in Hausa *takaba*, the traditional mourning period, with what is called "a sitting," although some of the widows are allowed to search for the resources needed to perform the burial of their husbands.[73] In northern Nigeria, the widow is not allowed to go anywhere in search of resources for her husbands' burial. To ensure she does not go out, her physical appearance is tarnished. For instance, the widow's hair is scraped off, and black cloth is tied to her head.[74] In places where her hair is not scraped off, the widow is instructed to ensure she does not look attractive to people.[75] In northern Nigeria, the colors of the mourning dress are black and white. Widows are expected to be dressed in black clothes until the mourning period is over. And it must be the same

---

68. Iheanacho, "Alienation of Nigerian Women," 21.
69. Iheanacho, "Alienation of Nigerian Women," 22.
70. Okoye, *Widowhood*, 2.
71. Iheanacho, "Alienation of Nigerian Women," 25.
72. Alumka, *Who Is a Widow?*
73. Rosenblatt and Nkosi, "South African Zulu Widows," 77.
74. Okoye, *Widowhood*, 49.
75. Okoye, *Widowhood*, 49.

dress widows wear for the mourning period, which lasts several months.[76] A white dress is worn after the completion of the mourning ritual. In other places, widows are not permitted to bathe, while in other places, widows are only allowed to bathe once a week.[77]

While some cultures in northern Nigeria do not require a dress code, they demand other things in its place, such as cooking for the crowd of mourners and wearing no make-up.[78] There are places in northern Nigeria where a widow wears a *bento*, a loincloth that was placed around the waist of her deceased husband. She is to wear it for three months. The outing ceremony to commemorate the end of the mourning period involves the shaving of hair and having bands tied around her head. There are widows who literally wear sacks and grass crowns or just a cloth on their heads. The widow only gets to start wearing what she likes after the outing ceremony.[79]

In some places within northern Nigeria, the first stage of mourning lasts for eight days. The second stage occurs several days later, in some cases thirty to forty days after the man's death. At this stage, the widow can move around her compound, but not beyond it. Then, the final stage takes place between six and twelve months after the husband's death. This involves cooking, drinking, eating, and merrymaking.

Widows in northern Nigeria are expected to complete the mourning ritual to gain their freedom to move around.[80] The widows embrace the mourning rituals because they believe it is divinely initiated and directed. For instance, Gloria, who has remarried, attributes her new identity, post-mourning ritual, to God. She states: "If I am not grateful to God for my life as a widow, then I do not know anything."[81] In other words, she is grateful for undergoing the widowhood mourning rituals because Gloria is convinced that God has led her to her present reality. While it is hard to gauge how the mourning ritual impacts her view of life now, she is expressing her agency as a staff member at EWS.

What I have done is briefly describe the mourning rituals in northern Nigeria. Mourning rituals provide continuity with the causes of the deaths of widows' husbands. But, as I said, the continuity is not to vindicate the

76. Okoye, *Widowhood*, 45.
77. Okoye, *Widowhood*, 49.
78. Okoye, *Widowhood*, 45, 49.
79. Okoye, *Widowhood*, 52–53.
80. Okoye, *Widowhood*, 43.
81. Gloria, interview by author, April 24, 2017.

widows from their husbands' deaths. Neither do I believe it is to liberate them from their death husbands' grips; rather, the mourning rituals are connected to rite of passage for widows. I discuss the combination of local rituals and Christian rites later in the chapter as I underscore the pertinent role Christianity must play in the agency of Christian widows. Therefore, while several factors have been proposed for what influences widowhood practices in Africa;[82] I suggest that the overarching factor is that widowhood mourning rituals are connected to rite of passage for widows in northern Nigeria. In other words, widowhood depicts a religious process that marks a pertinent stage in the widow's life.

Widowhood as a Rite of Passage

Victor Turner notes that Arnold van Gennep held that every rite of passage goes through three phases: *separation*, which constitutes symbolic behavior heralding the detachment of the group or individual either from an earlier established point in social structure and/or from a set of cultural conditions; *margin*, which involves passing through cultural sphere that has few or none of the characteristics of the past or future states; and *aggregation*, which refers to when the passage is achieved.[83] The widows' mourning rituals corresponds to Turner's phases since African widows go through a period of separation from accustomed environment, food, and bathing towards personhood.[84] Therefore, my proposal for a theology of embodiment involves the connection between mourning rituals and the rite of passage that engenders widow's agency towards a brighter future.[85] I return to the relationship between rituals and rites to discuss how this study uses the theme of Christianity and social change to propose a theology of embodiment.

Meanwhile, there is need to describe the liminal phase because Turner highlights it in his discussion on the rite of passage. Turner describes the liminal phase as ambiguous because it does not have the characteristics of the past or future phases.[86] Turner focuses on the liminal phase of the rite of passage because he believes it is the most ignored in the classifications

---

82. Okoye, *Widowhood*, 129–233.
83. Turner, *Ritual Process*, 94–95.
84. Edet, "Christianity and African Women's Rituals," 27.
85. Edet, "Christianity and African Women's Rituals," 31.
86. Turner, *Ritual Process*, 94.

that usually identify states in cultural space.[87] The liminal phase refers to "between" the state determined by customs.[88] Ngozi Iheanacho states that widows are located on the "indefinite threshold between life and death."[89] These widows transition to the future without any of the comforts they were accustomed to, while at the same time they are uncertain of the future. This makes this liminal phase the most difficult for the widows. It is important to describe the liminal phase of widowhood mourning rituals for two reasons: (1) the stories widows told stems from the ways the liminal phase shaped their lives; and (2) although most of the widows I interviewed had completed their rites of passages in widowhood, the contents of our conversations revolved around the liminal phases of their mourning rituals.

The Liminal Phase of Widowhood in Northern Nigeria

The liminal phase for a widow in northern Nigeria includes two major things. First, a widow is prevented from leaving the house because of her liminality of identity, the ritual mourning phase where she is removed from the familiar and thrust into the unknown "between." Rhoda's husband died a couple of months prior to our meeting. She told me she had not been out of the house for those two months.[90] This meant that she had not done most things she was once familiar with; neither had she seen several friends and family members. As one who existed in the "unknown," she was at the mercy of those who control the process of her rite of passage. Second, Rhoda was expected to be around people designated to her. She was scrutinized especially if she was seen interacting with men in public. She was considered a sexual risk to men. Some tribes in northern Nigeria believe the widow's interaction with men provokes the anger of the spirit of her dead husband.

Thus, Rhoda was supposed to be alienated from everyone other than those designated to her until after her outing ceremony.[91] However, her alienation affected her relationship with her children, who could not touch

---

87. Turner, *Ritual Process*, 95.
88. Turner, *Ritual Process*, 95.
89. Iheanacho, "Alienation of Nigerian Women," 205.
90. Rhoda, interview by author, March 27, 2017.
91. I was able to have an audience with her for two reasons: (1) She and I were not meeting in a public forum; and (2) others were present in the room. Thus, our meeting was strictly monitored.

her during the mourning period.[92] Rhoda's children kept a distance from her. What this means is that the role of the widow's family also becomes restricted under the demands of the widow's rites of passage. Deborah Bonat states that what makes the liminal phase most unbearable is the widow's inability to take care of her children the way she wants to.[93] While some of her family members stepped in to take care of her children, there were responsibilities that only Rhoda could provide for her children. But Rhoda was expected to live in isolation until her mourning ritual was completed.

What I have demonstrated above is that religious sentiments influence widows at every point of life. From the causes of their husbands' deaths to the mourning rituals that accompany widowhood, widows' lives are permeated by religious sentiments that determine the outcomes of widows' lived realities. I also noted that widowhood mourning rituals represent a rite of passage for Christian widows in northern Nigeria. In fact, rituals and rites are two religiously infused terminologies in northern Nigeria. What this means is that the connection between mourning rituals and the widows' rite of passage demonstrates the place of religion in widows' experiences. According to Oduyoye, religion accords a prime position to rites of passage associated with mourning rituals within Africa.[94] The combination of rituals and rites is pertinent to this research because it enhances the interaction between Christianity and social change in northern Nigeria.

Christianity and Social Change in Northern Nigeria

As I noted in the introduction of this study, my empirical research and the literature research show a strong link between religion and social change. Therefore, I want to show how the interaction between Christianity and social change happens. This is pertinent because this study is fundamentally about the interaction between the theological and social sciences. Thus, I examine social change from a theological perspective. Emmanuel Katongole also situates his discussion on social change within African religious sentiments. What Katongole demonstrates is the important interaction between Christianity and social change.

The interaction between Christianity and social change highlights the combination of local rituals and Christian rites. Christianity in northern

---

92. Oduyoye, "Women and Ritual," 15.
93. Bonat, "Challenges of Widowhood," 2.
94. Oduyoye, "Women and Ritual," 11.

Nigeria is a combination of local rituals and Christian rites. Given the pertinent role of Christianity in the social realities of widows in northern Nigeria, the combination of local rituals and Christian rites is inevitable. Ngozi Iheanacho describes the relationship between mourning rituals and Christian rites when she said widows are required to undergo rituals of separation and rites of reintegration towards a better future.[95] It is my position that the combination of local rituals and Christian rites is pertinent towards the agency of Christian widows in northern Nigeria.

However, the challenge is how widowhood rituals and Christian rites will lead to positive changes within northern Nigeria. As I noted, the widows understand that the social change that is brokered by religion is not easily managed or reversed. My respondents recognize that the interaction between religion and social change leads to either positive or negative social changes in society. Because of the important role Christianity plays towards the agency of Christian widows for social change, there is need to discuss how Christianity negatively and positively engenders the agency of Christian widows. In other words, there is need to discover some of the areas where the interaction between the social and theological provide challenges and avenues for social change.

Christianity and Negative Social Change

In his book *Christianity, Development and Modernity in Africa*, Paul Gifford examines the profound impact of religion on development efforts in Africa.[96] Gifford argues that religion plays a leading role in development, but this happens irregularly. He critiques different kinds of Christianities on the continent. Gifford confronts Pentecostalism for its religious imagination that blames everything on spiritual forces and ignores structural issues. And he criticizes Catholicism as nothing other than an NGO without using its theology to engage in development. Fundamentally, he criticizes patron-client relationships for much of Africa's underdevelopment.

The irregular role that religion plays in development is evident in the lived realities of Christian widows in northern Nigeria. Bonat laments the church's complicity in the plight of widows whenever the church fails to interfere on behalf of a widow being maltreated by her in-laws.[97] As a mother

---

95. Iheanacho, "Alienation of Nigerian Women," 21–22.
96. Gifford, *Christianity, Development and Modernity*.
97. Deborah Bonat, interview by author, March 22, 2017.

Religion and Agency

of three, Fatima struggles to provide for her young children. Her in-laws took everything she had. Without formal education and marketable skills by which she could secure a well-paying job, Fatima makes a living working for people either on their farms or in their homes. Unfortunately, these are seasonal jobs; thus, she could go for months without work and without any money to provide for her children.[98] Fatima said that her church never visited or helped her during her time of need. Donna Pridham, a staff member at EWS, said that although churches provide help, "you might be surprised as to how little the church does for the widows."[99] What these two accounts demonstrate is that the irregular role churches play in development undermines the widows' agency towards social change. I should add that churches do not have the responsibility to meet widows' needs because widows think they should meet her needs. Rather, they have this responsibility because biblical injunctions instruct Christians to meet the needs of widows.

Several reasons can be given for why churches often play irregular roles towards the development of Christian widows, but I would note a couple here: most mainline churches in northern Nigeria tend to structure their ministries to attract international sponsorship; thereby these churches give attention to ministries that benefactors consider worthy of their monies. In short, these churches are driven more by material rather than spiritual gains.[100] This is not to say that Pentecostal churches in northern Nigeria do not try to position themselves in terms of international money. In fact, Family Worship Center, a Pentecostal church I discuss in chapter 4, relates to churches around the world. Therefore, Gifford's argument is valid that Christianity has often failed to provide sustainable developments within African societies. Nevertheless, Christian religious sentiments advocate for positive social change within society. Christianity has immense value for social change in northern Nigeria.

Christianity and Positive Social Change

In his article "African Christianities and the Politics of Development from Below," Afe Adogame demonstrates that the interpretation and valuation of development "from above" (i.e. from international organizations) can be both useful and enriching, but they are potentially disputable and

---

98. Fatima, interview by author, March 16, 2017.
99. Donna, interview by author, March 24, 2017.
100. Gifford, *Christianity, Development and Modernity*, 103.

delineating in comprehending indigenous epistemologies and in developmental procedures, programs, and models in Africa.[101] Therefore, Adogame teased out how everyday lived religious dimensions of African life are pertinent to the understanding of development in the continent. In short, Adogame argues that economic and social indicators for measuring development should be accompanied by the "religious."

Adogame's contention is that churches are important in helping to empower Fatima towards social change. Adogame concurs with Gifford that churches can hinder positive social change.[102] Nevertheless, Adogame maintains that churches can both meet widows' needs and guide the agency of Christian widows.[103] In other words, churches can position these widows to become the prophetic voices that oppose faulty institutional systems of patron-client. Even Gifford's critique of the failure of churches to engineer the types of transformations Africa needs does not oppose the pertinent role that Christianity plays towards social change. Most importantly, Christian widows in northern Nigeria believe that religion is pertinent towards their agency. When the widows speak about God as their "husband," they do not mince words about where their faith and hope lie.[104] Even two Muslim widows I interviewed attest to the fact that organizations like GAWON more effectively meet widows' needs.[105] What their testimony demonstrates is that Christianity positively engenders the agency of Christian widows. In fact, Christianity has the best chance of implanting new modes of life and practices within Africa's old structures.[106]

In sum, Christianity negatively and positively engenders the agency of Christian widows. Churches have often played irregular roles towards engendering widows' agency. Consequently, widows are further marginalized and not empowered towards agency for social change. However, Christianity is pertinent in empowering Christian widows towards agency that leads to social change. Christianity best implants new ways of life and practices within northern Nigeria. Therefore, even though churches often fail to play regular roles towards engendering widows' agency, Christianity's role is central towards engendering widows' agency in northern Nigeria.

101. Adogame, "African Christianities," 1–11.

102. Adogame, "African Christianities," 66.

103. Adogame, "African Christianities," 66. See also Ogedegbe, "Christian Religion as Tool," 245–49.

104. Sophia, interview by author, March 29, 2017.

105. Rahila and Hajaratu, interview by author, March 27, 2017.

106. Okoye, *Widowhood*, 153.

Religion and Agency

To conclude, allow me to connect what I have said to cosmology because spiritual antecedents are so important to what I have said in this chapter. Because God is male within African cosmology, men in northern Nigeria assume a similarly superior role to God. Therefore, feminist theologians advocate for a neutral or feminine gender when referring to God.[107] Furthermore, since God has power over the physical and spiritual dimensions of life, men in northern Nigeria who assume a position like God within their homes also have power to control the material and spiritual affairs of their homes. What this mean is that women have no power to wield to effect change. Also, because God has intermediaries who are an extension of God, boys are groomed to extend the lineage of men. In fact, a major reason for polygamy is the search for a male child. Moreover, when Africans speak of "ancestors," the reference is largely to male ancestors. This relates to the next point about the anthropological nature of cosmology, where God is said to serve man's needs. Unmistakably, it is males that benefit from God's blessings. Therefore, religion becomes a tool towards marginalization of women, particularly widows.

However, given the important place of religion in the lives of widows, I propose that Christianity best empowers these widows towards agency despite the challenges of patrilineality. Their faith in Jesus enables Christian widows in northern Nigeria to redefine their widowhood. Beatrice Akua Duncan demonstrates the role wives play in the expansion and development of cocoa farms in some communities within Ghana.[108] Building on novel literature that demonstrates the potent interactions between marriage, land tenure relations, wives' labor, and cocoa in southern Ghana, Duncan shows that the interactions between these realities have augmented and assumed new and disparate dimensions. One of the results of this interaction is a strong link between cocoa production and conjugal union in mainly patrilineal societies. In other words, because men own the land, male cocoa farmers hire women for their productive engagement and reproductive aspect. To address this result, Duncan proposes an urgent need to engage communities in dialogue to arrive at a more suitable and acceptable property distribution pattern in marriage and on intestate death.[109]

But Duncan reveals that women are steering the conversation about what is "suitable" for them within patrilineal societies. Duncan shows that

107. Johnson, *She Who Is*.
108. Duncan, "Cocoa, Marriage, Labour and Land," 301–21.
109. Duncan, "Cocoa, Marriage, Labour and Land," 317–18.

women are not waiting for those dialogues to happen. Duncan notes that women within the Ghanaian communities she researched accept support for children's education instead of land or farm resources.[110] In other words, women are more interested in carrying out their agency as mothers and wives than being consigned to their stereotypical gender roles within African societies. Duncan describes this as a "recent shift" within the communities she researched in Ghana. However, I demonstrate that this shift is not recent for Christian widows in northern Nigeria. Christian widows in northern Nigeria have been redefining their widowhood. Strongly believing that they have religious, economic, and social agency, Christian widows in northern Nigeria are resisting remarriage and property inheritance if it undermines their ability to become agents of social change. As most of the literature on African widows that focus on remarriage and property inheritance, Duncan appeals for a more suitable property distribution for African women. Nevertheless, the dialogues needed in African societies should move beyond just issues of remarriage or acquiring property for widows; rather, what Christian widows in northern Nigeria demand is for the dialogues to focus more on the agency of widows towards social change.

Conclusion

The context of northern Nigeria demonstrates strong religious sentiments. In describing the history of northern Nigeria, it becomes clear that religious sentiments shape widows' experiences. From marriage to their widowhood, religion has been used to disempower widows. Moreover, religious sentiments undergird both the causes of the deaths of widows' husbands and the mourning rituals by making widows responsible for their husbands' deaths. However, the interaction between religion and social change engenders the combination of local rituals and Christian rites that positions widows to become agents of social change. What this underscores is the need for continuous interaction between Christianity and cultural practices to address elements that undermine the widows' agency in northern Nigeria. Building upon this chapter, the following chapters demonstrate that theological resources are pertinent to the agency of Christian widows in northern Nigeria. The next chapter shows that theological resources enhance greater religious, social, and economic agency of Christian widows in northern Nigeria.

110. Duncan, "Cocoa, Marriage, Labour and Land," 301.

3

Religious, Economic, and Social Agency

ON A HOT, STEAMY day in March 2017, I met with six Christian widows for a focus group session at GAWON. There were three veteran widows and three young widows. They all wore colorful dresses and headscarves. Their jewelry ranged from necklaces to bangles and earrings. Their demeanor can simply be expressed as "anxious" because they seemed uneasy about my presence. But the anxieties faded as the conversation progressed. The veteran widows were more loquacious than the young widows. They shared stories about their challenges as widows, particularly the burden of raising their children alone without marketable skills or formal education to secure well-paying jobs. They narrated their heart-wrenching stories of maltreatment, isolation, and poverty.

The young widows also shared their challenges. Binta steered our conversation by directly asking me whether she should remarry. She is a mother who is struggling to raise her three children. She said a man had proposed marriage to her, and she was considering it. I posed the question to the older widows. Very soon, a conversation ensued between the veteran and young widows about remarriage. The first question the veteran widows asked Binta was, "Is he going to take care of you *and* the children?" She gave a reluctant yes. The two other young widows also spoke about the difficulty of remarriage because men were not interested in taking care of their five children. (Both of them have five children each.) The veteran widows underscored the need to marry someone willing to support both the young widows *and* their children. The young widows listened attentively to the veterans, occasionally wiping tears from their faces.

For fifteen minutes, the veterans counseled and encouraged the young widows. I only interrupted to clarify points they raised. When we concluded our session, the veteran widows asked to speak privately with the young widows. So I left the room. I recall how uplifted the young widows were after their private session. I overheard one young widow telling someone, "The veteran widows listened to us, and advised us on what we needed to do." I realized I had just witnessed the agency of Christian widows in northern Nigeria.

My argument in this chapter is that faith engenders greater religious, economic, and social agency towards social change. I demonstrate what the widows have accomplished towards social change in northern Nigeria. Then, I explore how faith enhances greater achievements of widows by addressing the issue of "status." I suggest that widows' roles as wives and mothers position widows to effect social change. What I demonstrate is that widows' agency arises from limited religious, economic, and social resources that are characteristic of widowhood.

First, if the widows believe their roles as wives and mothers are agentic, then it means these widows have contributed to the religious, economic, and social dimensions of northern Nigeria. In other words, they exercised agency with the little power they had before becoming widows. A brief investigation into the religious, economic, and social agency of these widows is warranted here as I explore Christian widows' agency.

Women's Contributions toward Social Change in Northern Nigeria

Economically, women make up the largest labor force in food production in Africa.[1] Patrycja Kozieł provides a unique perspective on the lives of women in northern Nigeria, addressing their rights and daily challenges.[2] Kozieł states that more than 50 million women in Nigeria live and work in rural areas, where they provide 60–79 percent of the rural labor force and make a living from the land.[3]

1. Mutume, "African Women Battle for Equality."
2. Kozieł, "Hausa Women's Rights," 217–29.
3. Kozieł, "Hausa Women's Rights," 217–29.

Religious, Economic, and Social Agency

Socially, the fact that women outlive men in northern Nigeria suggests that women play a more significant role in the socio-political structure than people realize.[4] Women give birth to children, societies' potential leaders. Moreover, it is not only fathers who bless their children; mothers, too, can bestow blessings. This is especially the case when the widow is the only parent the children have. Therefore, women in northern Nigeria have contributed to society by raising their children alone.

Religiously, women provide important services that legitimize the existence of northern Nigerian deities.[5] What I mean is that women participate in religious activities that keep deities relevant within northern Nigeria. Even outside of northern Nigerian deities, women contribute significantly to religious agency around the country. As critical agents of religion, women practice Christianity more than men do.[6] Women make up most Christians in the global South and are critical to the growth of new churches across northern Nigeria.[7] Women are the backbone of most rural churches in northern Nigeria.[8]

Thus, northern Nigerian women have contributed to the region's economic, social, and religious realities. Their contributions to the sustainability of the region in these important aspects of life cannot be overemphasized. The northern Nigerian woman is regarded for her business acumen, her civility, and her faith. As Nigeria steers its economy towards agriculture, the northern Nigerian woman's participation is vital for mass production. As Nigeria pursues peace, the northern Nigerian woman can mediate and usher in the era of peace in the country. And as Nigeria encourages its citizens to pray for spiritual revivals, it is to the northern Nigerian woman that they look to for inspiration.

Since the widows have expressed agency before becoming widows, this provides an important backdrop towards discussing the ways towards greater agency. Thus, Christian women have achieved religious, economic, and social agency; however, what I am suggesting in this chapter is that faith engenders even greater religious, economic, and social agency of Christian widows. What the veteran widows above demonstrate is that Christianity

---

4. CIA, "Nigeria."
5. Motty, *Indigenous Christian Disciple-Making*, 237.
6. Hastings, *World History of Christianity*, 225.
7. Hastings, *World History of Christianity*, 246.
8. Hastings, *A World History of Christianity*, 226.

gives widows the right to decide their lives in freedom.⁹ In other words, God accords widows the status necessary to achieve greater religious, economic, and social agency.

The Status of Christian Widows

Even though widows have once expressed agency, widowhood undermines the widow's religious, economic, and social agency within society. Society no longer sees them as wives or mothers. That society no longer regards widows as wives and mothers raises the issue of status. The status of widows is a contested one in northern Nigeria. In his article "Widows in Hausa Society: Ritual Phase or Social Status?", Enid Schildkrout argues that among the people of northern Nigeria, widowhood is a ritual phase and not a visible social status.[10] What Schildkrout means is that the African widow does not have an official status.[11] By "official," Schildkrout refers to the status society confers upon African women. But the anthropological volume in which Schildkrout's article appears fails to consider the religious aspect of widowhood, which is essential to sustaining the status of African widows. By "religious aspect," I am referring to my point that God accords widows' status to effect social change. Recognizing the religious aspect of widowhood, Cheryl Pridham, registrar at EWS, stated: "Widows have a social status. The problem is their social status as widows does not enhance anything."[12]

Schildkrout and Pridham might disagree on whether widows have status. However, their conclusions suggest that whether widows have status or not, the widows do not effect social change. Patrycja Kozieł's recent study in northern Nigeria also demonstrate that a widow's status enhances nothing in her life or society.[13] Pridham points out that widows' inability to enhance anything is due to the ways that society treats them. When I asked Binta about the agency of widows, her response was, "the widow becomes like *kashi* (excrement) in society." Lillian, a middle-aged widow commenting on the experiences of widows, agreed with Binta: *An yi banza da mu* ("we are rendered worthless").[14] In other words, society imposes societal

---

9. Beya, "Human Sexuality," 177.
10. Schildkrout, "Widows in Hausa Society?" 131–52.
11. Oduyoye, "Women and Ritual," 16.
12. Cheryl Pridham, interview by author, March 24, 2017.
13. Kozieł, "Hausa Women's Rights," 217.
14. Lillian, interview by author, March 2, 2017.

rules upon widows that deny widows the "official status" to effect social change. Most importantly, what this also shows is that society refuses to recognize the status God accords widows to effect social change.

The reason the veteran widows encouraged the young widows to see their widowhood as a divine charge towards agency is to remind them of their God-given status that demands their agency. The veteran widows recognize the pertinent roles widows must play towards social change. Madugu, a staff member at GAWON, said, "If we want to develop our communities, we must engage the widows."[15] Madugu's statement is based on the premise that God has positioned widows to effect social change. Therefore, when I speak of widows' roles as wives and mothers, I share Cheryl and Madugu's sentiment that God has given widows the status they need as wives and mothers to effect social change. Therefore, my aim in this chapter is to explore how widows' God-given status positions them to achieve greater religious, social, and economic agency within society as they carry out their roles as wives and mothers.

Before I proceed, I should note the resistance from feminist theologians against the notion that only through their roles as wives and mothers can African women contribute to the development of society.[16] I acknowledge that the roles of wives and mothers are not the only ways widows can express agency. In fact, I show that the widows' roles as wives and mothers have ever-expanding agency within society. I also show in this study that widows expressed ambition to become educators, politicians, and missionaries. Thus, the roles of wives and mothers are only a part of their broader agency. However, the overwhelming response from all my respondents is that widows' roles as wives and mothers are divinely mandated roles that position them to effect greater social change. I describe the widows' roles as wives and mothers before discussing how their faith engenders their religious, economic, and social agency.

The Widow as Wife in Northern Nigeria

When Janet's husband was still alive, they lived in a family compound with her in-laws. Her marriage into the family meant she was responsible for everything that her aging mother-in-law could not do. So, Janet cooked, cleaned, sewed, knitted, went to the market, fetched water, and washed. She

15. Madugu Nuhu Idi, interview by author, March 27, 2017.
16. Oduyoye, *Daughters of Anowa*, 178.

assumed the role of "wife" to the entire family. When her husband died, she remained in the house, fulfilling her role as a wife.[17] Culturally, Janet was not obligated to stay. She remained because, according to her, "African marriage contract makes my husband's family my primary family."[18] This is true across northern Nigeria, where a woman's in-laws refer to her as *matanmu* ("our wife"). Feminist theologians such as Oduyoye would not support Janet's decision because they hold that marriage can undermine the woman's agency.[19] But Janet believes remaining was what God wanted her to do. Thus, while other factors might have influenced her decision to remain, it was ultimately her faith in God that inspired her to remain with her in-laws. She considers the praise she has earned from her community as confirmation that it was God's intention for her to remain with her in-laws. Therefore, Janet would disagree with Oduyoye that her decision undermines her agency; rather, she suggests that God has used her devotion to enhance her agency.

Even widows who do not choose to remain with their in-laws show devotion in a different way. Jummai refused to remarry when her husband died. Rather, she focused on raising her children. She witnessed them graduate, marry, and secure good jobs. When I visited Jummai at her home, I observed that after several years since her husband's death, his photos still adorn the walls of their home. It is unclear if Jummai shares the sentiments of her Luo counterparts about being a "wife of the grave,"[20] but it might provide some explanations for the presence of her husband's photos in her home. Jummai still aids her late husband's family in various ways. For instance, she financially supports her husband's niece, who is in boarding school. She considers it her God-honoring responsibility to take care of "my husband's family."[21] Note she did not say "my late husband's

---

17. This raises the question of levirate marriages. What she describes does not align with levirate customs that require the relative of the deceased husband to inherit the wife. In Janet's case, it seems like there were agreements between her and the in-laws about arrangements. Her situation seems to support Betty Potash's view about widows who make decisions for themselves (Potash, *Women in African Societies*). Thus, she is not forced into a levirate marriage, but chooses to remain with her husband's family to fulfill her roles as the family's "wife." Again, this is rare, and there is simply no precedence for it. Some families are engaged in transforming practices, however.

18. Janet, interview by author, April 10, 2017.
19. Oduyoye, *Daughters of Anowa*, 67.
20. Kirwen, *African Widows*, 36.
21. Jummai, interview by author, March 24, 2017.

family," because she believes there is continuity of status as wife beyond her husband's death.

I should note that Janet and Jummai's devotion should not be seen as fear of misfortune if they remarry.[22] These widows have concluded their mourning rituals; thus, they are free from any obligation to their husbands or their husbands' families. What motivates their agency is the belief that their roles as wives are an unbreakable bond because marriage is established by God himself. In Jummai's case, for instance, the photos indicate that the "family" extends into the past and future. This is supported by the cosmological view that human interaction with God includes the souls of those who have died. In other words, these widows' commitments to their husband's families are inspired by the held beliefs that marriage is a deeply religious arrangement in northern Nigeria. Michael Kirwen also adds that marriage establishes wider social ties that extend to the dead.[23] Therefore, religion perpetuates the widows' role as "wives" within society. In short, their agency towards their husbands' families is inspired by their resilient faith in God.

The Widow as Mother in Northern Nigeria

Oduyoye puts the role of the African woman thus: "The aura of life and 'livingness' that surrounds the woman is the center of the home, and a woman is assumed to be faithfully motherly."[24] The role of an African mother is to fulfill her biological roles, care for the children, feed, train, and discipline them.[25] Thus, every woman in northern Nigeria, for instance, is a mother who contributes to the progress of everyone.

Theresa's story provides a complex perspective on a widow as a mother. Theresa is in her third year as a student at EWS. She is not just a widow but has never had children of her own. Theresa was one of six widows I accompanied to the market one day. On our way back from the market, two teenage girls stopped to greet Theresa. They called her *Ma* (a title given to matriarchs in northern Nigeria). In a culture where bearing children is fundamental to life[26] and a woman is defined as "she who bears children,"

---

22. Oduyoye, *Daughters of Anowa*, 67.
23. Kirwen, *African Widows*, 40.
24. Oduyoye, *Daughters of Anowa*, 60.
25. Oduyoye, *Daughters of Anowa*, 59.
26. Oduyoye, *Daughters of Anowa*, 81.

the greetings she received from the teenage girls authenticated her role as a mother within society. The girls' greetings also underscore the fact that Theresa has a wider role as a mother in society because motherhood is a divinely mandated role for every woman in northern Nigeria.

The role of mother that Theresa has is supported by Felicia's comment that *Yaro ba na mutum daya bane ya rike* ("A child is not only for one person to raise").[27] Therefore, every woman is a potential mother to every child in northern Nigeria because that is what God sanctioned. What this means is that even Theresa is responsible for helping to raise the next generation. Oduyoye states that widows such as Theresa can support their procreating sisters in several ways, including instructing the children.[28] To nurture the next generation is a communal responsibility, and every woman of the community becomes one's mother.[29]

In sum, the role of wives and mothers are divinely mandated for every woman in northern Nigeria to assume. Widows believe that God positions them towards greater achievements as mothers and wives in society. What this underscore is that faith is pertinent to the agency of Christian widows in northern Nigeria. I am now going to examine how faith enhances the religious, economic, and social agency of widows towards social change. Specifically, my goal is to demonstrate that faith enables widows to provide greater religious, economic, and social achievements towards social change in northern Nigeria.

Enhancing Greater Religious, Economic, and Social Agency

Widows contribute significantly towards social change through their religious, economic, and social agency. Oduyoye states that development studies have been incomplete due to Western writers' failure to connect the agency of West African women in local socio-economies to the religious dimensions of African societies.[30] There are two implications to Oduyoye's statement. First, the religious, economic, and social dimensions of life are intertwined.[31] And, second, the widows' faith undergirds widows' religious,

27. Felicia, interview by author, March 23, 2017.
28. Oduyoye, *Daughters of Anowa*, 81.
29. Oduyoye, *Daughters of Anowa*, 26.
30. Oduyoye, *Daughters of Anowa*, 11.
31. I stated earlier in the study that the widows did not differentiate between "religion" and "faith," and I will continue to use the terms interchangeably at times. However,

Religious, Economic, and Social Agency

social, and economic agency. By that, I mean faith engenders widows' religious, economic, and social agency in northern Nigeria, and faith provides widows the religious, economic, and social resources necessary to effect significant change in northern Nigeria.

At EWS and GAWON, faith undergirds the religious, economic, and social agency of Christian widows. This is not surprising, because Nigerians have amazing religious impulses.[32] What I mean is that faith is central to life in northern Nigeria. For this reason, EWS and GAWON are using the Christian faith as a basis for their development programs. Cheryl Pridham insists that the "spiritual aspect" is the most important part of the widows' training at EWS.[33] Also, Micah, the program manager at GAWON states, "The Christian faith is the driving force behind all we do."[34] The biblical training EWS and GAWON provide the widows underscores the pertinent role of faith in the agency of widows.

Ninety percent of the widows from EWS and GAWON referenced God/Lord/Jesus/Christ without being prodded by me or anyone.[35] Most of these references to God were done in prayerful postures, but other times it flowed through their conversations with me and with each other. Overwhelmingly, the widows referred to God as *mai taimakona* ("my helper"), expressing both gratitude and trust in God. Their faith in God positions them to effect social change in every aspect of life. By that, I mean the widows believe that widowhood is a divine charge towards agency that leads to social change.[36] What the descriptions below demonstrate is that faith does not only demand widows' religious, economic, and social agency, faith plays a key role towards widows' religious, economic, and social agency. In describing the religious, economic, and social agency of widows, I state the need for widows' agency, the role of faith in widows' agency, and ways widows express their agency towards social change.

I would use the terms separately to avoid conflating widows' personal convictions from religion as a social phenomenon in northern Nigeria.

32. Adogame, "God Became a Nigerian," 479–98.
33. Cheryl Pridham, interview by author, March 24, 2017.
34. Micah, interview by author, March 27, 2017.
35. It would be wrong to conclude that the widows who did not mention God during the interviews did not believe in God. In fact, both asked for prayers—one for her children and the other for another widow whose plight she said was worse than hers.
36. Dina, interview by author, April 30, 2017.

Agents of Social Change

Religious Agency of Christian Widows

In *My Faith as an African,* Jean-Marc Ela argues that allowing Africans to change Christian traditions into familiar and useful forms is the only way to restore their dignity.[37] For instance, he suggests that the Eucharist should be served with local rather than imported products. Ela suggests that biblical interpretation should be patterned by what he calls "shade-tree theology," where small cohorts of Christians get together to interpret the Bible considering their own situations. Their religious agency depends on their ability to participate in the theologizing process. Unfortunately, African widows are prevented from participating in the articulation of an African theology that is faithful to the Bible and relevant to their lives. Thus, despite their religious agency in the past, widows are not welcome under the theologizing tree. Their absence at the shade tree undermines their religious resources necessary to effect social change. The widows' faith demands their participation in African religious life.

The Role of Faith in the Religious Agency of Christian Widows

Because the widows' faith demands their religious agency, there is need to describe the role faith plays in the religious agency of Christian widows in northern Nigeria. Ela deals with the questions of faith posed by cultural variables, an internal dimension of the African's condition. In other words, what Ela's approach suggests is that faith is central to African life. Ela suggests that the basic issue of the reality of Christianity is being raised from within the dynamic which allows Africans to escape from the inhumanity of the destiny to which certain factors would condemn them. According to Ela, a critical reflection on the relevance of an African Christianity requires us to identify the structures or strategies of exploitation and impoverishment against which Africans have always struggled to find their own specific forms of religious agency.

I also draw upon *Development and Politics from Below* to underscore the expanding principle role religion plays in Africa.[38] In his article "Health and Uses of Religion: Recovering the Political Proper?" James R. Cochrane's analysis uses the history and recent state of public health states as a framework for analyzing current research on the role of faith in health systems.

---

37. Ela, *My Faith as an African.*
38. Bompani and Frahm-Arp, *Development and Politics.*

Of importance to this study, Cochrane states that religion in developing countries is a reservoir of political autonomy, moral authority, and moral education, and is a major factor in the motivation of people.[39] In other words, faith is crucial to the realities of Africans because it enables people to live their lives in freedom.

Ela and Cochrane highlight the role of faith in the agency of Africans. What Cochrane underscores is that faith is pertinent towards carrying out the specific forms of agency Ela envisions Africans need to overcome the structures that undermine their agency. What I draw from Cochrane's and Ela's conclusions is that faith is pertinent towards the religious agency of widows. In reflecting on the relevance of their Christian faith, the widows are convinced that God "chose" them to become widows. During a focus group session with fifteen widows, Favor narrated her story of widowhood. Her husband died after a brief illness, leaving her with three children to raise. She said it was strange being a widow because her mother was also a widow. Looking back, she credits her mother's faith in raising them. And she also credits EWS for helping to strengthen her faith in God, which positions her to effect social agency. To this, she repeated Theresa Adamu's sentiment that widowhood is a calling.[40] I asked the fourteen other widows in the room, "How many of you feel that widowhood is a calling?" With firm head-nods and raised of hands, they all agreed. This further explains why the veteran widows admonished the young widows to see their widowhood as a divine charge towards agency that leads to social change.[41]

As I noted, the widows' references to God are strongly connected to prayer. It is safe to assert that prayer is the primary calling of Christian widows in northern Nigeria. In fact, prayer grounds every agency of Christian widows. When asked how they would transform Nigeria, the widows overwhelmingly said, "Pray for Nigeria." Comfort said, "I need to pray for Nigeria because God hears the prayers of a widow." When widows in northern Nigeria pray, their prayers are largely for the transformation of Nigeria. In GAWON, there is a group of widows that meets specifically to pray. One

---

39. Cochrane, "Health and Uses of Religion," 181.

40. Favor, interview by author, March 16, 2017.

41. My reservations for pushing the line of thinking that widowhood is a calling is that it can be misconstrued in a couple of ways: either a widow might think herself better than someone because God entrusted her with widowhood, or it can be self-defeating, especially for young widows who might face opposition or refuse to remarry, even if that is the right course of action. But this bespeaks the influence that faith exerts on the religious agency of Christian widows in northern Nigeria.

of the first members of that prayer group was Salome. Her husband died and left her with seven children. She also lost two children after her husband's death. She joined the prayer group as a young new widow and has remained connected to the group in her old age. Salome believes that "the prayer of a widow can transform society."[42]

With prayer as a foreground, the widows believe that they are specifically called to raise godly children that would transform their society. This concurs with Enid Schildkrout's point that northern Nigerians believe biological and social paternity must coincide.[43] Comfort, a young widow, said, "If I neglect my children, they would become a nuisance to society."[44] Several widows, including Comfort, refer to their children as *amana daga Allah* ("a trust from God"). What this means is that God has called widows to ensure that the children God gave them also become agents of social change themselves. However, while the widows readily connected raising godly children to transforming society, I consider them separately below to demonstrate widows' ever-expanding roles as wives and mothers within society.

Raising Godly Children

When Gina's husband died, he left her with three children. They were living in the family compound with some of her husband's relatives. Upon his death, her in-laws told her to leave the house. She refused. And then the maltreatment began. At first, it was emotional maltreatment (i.e., isolation, mocking, and threats). Very soon, the physical abuse followed (i.e., beatings). She fled to her parents when her-laws threatened her life. But she returned three days later. She said, "I worried about my children. I worried about what they were eating. I'd rather die knowing they are safe."[45] However, the greater motivation to return was that Gina was responsible for raising them in a godly way, according to the Bible. Therefore, she did not want to fail in fulfilling her divine mandate of raising children that can transform society. In her case, Bonat had five daughters she successfully raised, choosing not to remarry when her husband died even though she was a young widow. She said, "I had five daughters; and I chose to focus on

---

42. Salome, interview by author, March 28, 2017.
43. Schildkrout, "Widows in Hausa Society?" 151.
44. Comfort, interview by author, March 29, 2017.
45. Gina, interview by author, March 24, 2017.

training them."⁴⁶ It would be misguided to think that "training" only refers to secular education. Bonat was emphatic that biblical training is foundational to positioning widows to raise godly children. Gina also talked about how the biblical training she received at EWS prepared her to train her children towards godly lifestyles that can transform society.

Widows like Gina are rising to the challenge regarding raising godly children. Widows in northern Nigeria symbolize society's hopes because they are responsible for raising society's future leaders. Some churches in northern Nigeria recognize this as well. Musa, an elder in one of the churches where most of the widows have membership, said that over 50 percent of the homes in the community were managed by widows.⁴⁷ According to him, these widows embrace their religious agency to raise godly children. Thus, Musa noted that the church was aware of the important role that widows have in raising godly children for society, and in turn, transforming society.

Transforming Society

As a mother to her children, the widow is also responsible for raising godly children according to the needs of society. Thus, she is to train her children to contribute positively to society. She provides her children with biblical instruction to prepare them to live responsibly within society. These children can transform society by their dedication to their professions. Thus, whether they become doctors or janitors, the widows' children are to contribute positively to social change because widows raised them properly.

But I chose to discuss "transforming society" separately to underscore the expanding agency of widows. Cochrane suggests that faith engenders social integration of women in African societies because the agency of "citizens" is expanding.⁴⁸ Bonat states that raising godly children who can contribute positively to society leads towards expansive avenues for agency.⁴⁹ Bonat travels the country to teach widows marketable skills such as making lotions, soaps, and snacks. She testifies that some of the widows she has encountered have taken her advice, using their skills to feed and nurture their communities. For instance, some of the widows have been hired as teachers in schools where they are influencing the lives of future generations.

46. Deborah Bonat, interview by author, March 22, 2017.
47. Musa, interview by author, April 25, 2017.
48. Cochrane, "Health and Uses of Religion," 175.
49. Deborah Bonat, interview by author, March 22, 2017.

Agents of Social Change

One of the ways Bonat wanted her children, the widows, and others she mentors to contribute positively to society is to champion justice for all people. By teaching them biblical principles, she anticipates that they can become advocates for others. Ela challenges the church to refuse the dogmas that perpetuate injustices against the poor. He asserts that the church needs to be relevant by meeting the real needs of people. Rephrasing the philosopher Jurgen Habermas, Cochrane presents faith as an idea of collective values.[50] By this, he states that religion is both generative and empowering of all people.[51] Bonat demonstrates the generative and empowering nature of faith through her religious agency. Together, Ela and Cochrane advocate for a faith that takes the issue of empowering others seriously. The implication is that, if given the opportunity, the widow's faith can be instrumental in transforming people's lives in society. Bonat insists that faith is the foundation towards expansive agency for widows. Therefore, she always tells widows, "There's no way you can live for Christ and not touch another person."[52] Thus, buoyed by their strong sense of calling, widows become agents of greater social change.

To conclude, since widows' religious agency is pertinent to social change, they must be included in the theologizing that is taking place within society. Ela's "shade tree theology" ensures that widows participate in interpreting the Bible considering their own situations. I understand that this is a radical proposition in a patriarchal context like northern Nigeria. But Ela suggests the need for what he terms an "ethics of transgression," a deliberate break with Western Christianities' hold on African Christians, that embraces cultural practices that align with the Bible. By proposing that widows participate in articulating an African theology, I am suggesting a kind of ethics of transgression because Christianity gives widows the right to decide their lives in freedom. Their faith engenders their religious agency of raising godly children that would, in turn, transform society.

In sum, faith undergirds the religious agency of widows. Widows believe God chose them to raise godly children and transform society, with prayer as a foundation. These areas of calling underscore the role that faith plays in the religious agency of Christian widows. The widows' areas of calling are also present in the conversation about positioning widows to effect social change in other aspects of life. By that, I mean prayer, raising

---

50. Cochrane, "Health and Uses of Religion," 181.
51. Cochrane, "Health and Uses of Religion," 181–82.
52. Deborah Bonat, interview by author, March 22, 2017.

godly children, and transforming society feature in the widows' economic and social agency in northern Nigeria. I turn now to discussing how faith undergirds the widows' economic agency.

Economic Agency of Christian Widows

African children have depended on food produced by subsistence farming done largely by women.[53] Traditionally, African women have farmed, traded, processed, prepared, and sold food, made pottery, woven and dyed cloth, and made it into wearing apparel.[54] However, widows like Hajara do not have economic resources that enhance their economic agency. In other words, despite their economic agency in the past, widows have limited access to economic resources. Their economic agency depends on their ability to access those resources. Nevertheless, widows persist in carrying out their economic agency because faith demands their participation in African economic life.

When Hajara's husband died, she was left to fend for her seven children alone. Like many widows I interviewed, Hajara possesses no skill to secure a well-paying job. And this means she has limited to no financial resources. She does not only have her children but still must provide for her grandchildren as well because one of her married sons moved back home due to poor health. Hajara thus bears the financial burden for ten people. She said, "We wake up every day not knowing where our meal would come from."[55] She does not only need money for food, but she also needs money to pay the rent of the two-bedroom apartment she shares with ten other people. All she has is a little farm where she grows enough food to feed her family. Meanwhile, if she needs money for cooking ingredients, she begs her neighbors. Because widows like Hajara are expected to carry out economic roles as part of their mothering tasks,[56] widows desire to improve their economic standards towards agency.

---

53. United States Women's Bureau, "United Nations Decade for Women."
54. Oduyoye, *Daughters of Anowa*, 100.
55. Hajara, interview by author, March 16, 2017.
56. Oduyoye, *Daughters of Anowa*, 62.

Agents of Social Change

The Role of Faith in the Economic Agency of Christian Widows

The motivation behind Hassana's desire to improve her economic standard is her faith. Hassana said the urge to go to school to enable her to get a good job and provide for her family "felt like a message directly sent to my heart."[57] She believes that God has chosen her to make a difference through her economic agency. In fact, every widow at EWS strongly believes that it was God who led them to the school either through dreams, visions, convictions, or their pastors. The sense of calling I described above applies here too. Thus, despite the educational and skills acquisition programs EWS and GAWON offers, the widows' faith is pertinent to her economic agency. Attempts to help Hajara get a formal education or marketable skills are ineffective without the spiritual instruction required to sustain her economic agency. In other words, while she needs educational and marketable skills, Hajara's faith is pertinent towards her economic agency within society.

Hajara said her prayers "often sounded Pentecostal," which means they were spontaneous and vigorous. As their primary calling, prayer is also pertinent to widows' lives because the widows believe that their poverty is a spiritual battle. For instance, Hajara strongly believes that it is the devil's plot to keep her poor, so she turns to vigorous prayers. Paul Gifford says that such an "enchanted religious imagination" can hinder Hajara's development and erode her agency.[58] Rather, Gifford suggests a rational analysis to help Hajara. But, as I show below, Gifford's modernity does not position Christian widows to effect social change in northern Nigeria. Gifford's suggestion that Africans need to pull away from what he terms "enchanted Christianity" undermines the holistic development vision for Africa. In other words, such a sentiment ignores the ways widows draw from their faith towards economic agency. Thus, what is vital towards engendering Hajara's economic agency is her faith in God. She needs to believe that God will *taimake* ("help") her overcome the uphill battle she faces towards economic agency. She is positioned for agency when she draws from her faith to help her overcome the economic challenges she faces. In fact, faith ensures a greater achievement of her economic agency. Therefore, failure to recognize the role faith plays towards her agency undermines her agency. Exercising her faith in prayer and devotion positions her to contribute towards the economic realities of her society.

---

57. Hassana, interview by author, March 16, 2017.
58. Gifford, *Christianity, Development and Modernity*, 13.

Religious, Economic, and Social Agency

In conversations with my respondents, they spoke a lot about providing widows economic opportunities to position them to effect social change. Their responses highlighted two pertinent ways faith enables widows to express their economic agency. The respondents talked about the need for widows to provide fair economic environment for others. And the respondents also underscored the need to educate widows about supporting the education and skills acquisition of others. What I found fascinating was that my respondents did not just suggest that these are two ways widows are empowered towards agency; rather, all my respondents insisted that widows express their economic agency in these two ways.

Fair Economic Environment

As I noted, most widows do not have land to raise crops. But even if they have land to raise crops, they lack the capacity for high yield because of the economic manipulations of natural and human forces. What I mean is that even though the markets of West African states such as Nigeria are run by women, they are impacted by changing global climate, health challenges, and men who control much of what happens behind the scenes. Moreover, "middlemen" buy goods when the goods are plentiful to avoid paying high prices, and then they sell the goods at exorbitant prices when the goods become scarce. This has undermined widows' contributions to the economic dimensions of society. In short, their reality renders them incapable of farming, trading, processing, preparing, and selling food. For Hajara, this is a huge challenge because she has more mouths to feed than her little farm can provide. She still faces some natural forces such as drought since northern Nigeria is very dry all year around. And she also faces the human forces of middlemen who still control what happens behind the market scenes. These challenges undermine Hajara's ability to make profits towards greater economic agency.

To help widows, GAWON and EWS provide land for widows to grow food to feed their children and even others. By helping widows overcome some of the natural and human forces of poverty, the widows can not only grow food to feed their families but help other widows who are unable to overcome issues such as sickness. On her little farm, Hajara grows yams, taro, potato, and groundnut. With that, she feeds her children and helps other widows who do not have as much as she does. Obviously, the widows desire to provide for their children, since this aligns with their religious agency. But I was amazed by the widows who were concerned about other widows' well-being. During one of our focus group sessions, Abigail, a veteran widow, connected other widows to people who would help them secure loans to start small businesses.[59] And this is because someone helped her secure loans years ago to start her own business. She came to EWS because she faced some of the economic challenges Hajara experiences. Yet, she wants to help other widows gain a fairer economic environment. And, as I show, Abigail is not the only one concerned about the economic situations of other widows. In short, what widows asked for to achieve greater economic output is what they offer each other. The motivation behind their concern for each other is their faith in God. In other words, widows like Abigail share Bonat's sentiment that being a Christian involves helping someone.

But my respondents also talked about the need for education and skills acquisition for widows to overcome their economic challenges and engender their economic agency. Gifford proposes modern approaches to development that accord people education and marketable skills.[60] I agree with Gifford that Hajara needs education and marketable skills to navigate a mutating global economy. But it depends on what we mean by "modernity." For Gifford, African modernity is like the modernity in the West. In other words, Gifford believes the modernity that arose from the Enlightenment is the only type of modernity. But such an approach leaves the widow out of the process of her development and undermines her economic agency. Therefore, the modernity Gifford proposes will not position Christian widows in northern Nigeria towards economic agency that leads to social change. What I propose is the need to educate widows on how to draw upon Western and African motifs to effect social change. Such a position is behind my description of how education and acquiring marketable skills enables widows to embody economic agency.

Education and Skills Acquisition

Unfortunately, illiteracy is a common reality among many African women.[61] Hassana had no formal education before she got married. She started high school but had to drop out of school because her parents could not

---

59. Abigail, interview by author, March 31, 2017.

60. Gifford, *Christianity, Development and Modernity*, 85.

61. Okoye, *Widowhood*, 167. In northern Nigeria, a person is considered "illiterate" if they do not have formal education or have any marketable skills.

afford her school fees. She never went back to school but got married in her late teens. When her husband died, Hassana enrolled at EWS. She enrolled in computer-literacy classes to prepare her for well-paying jobs in a twenty-first-century world.[62] She is also taking the knitting, sewing, and cooking classes EWS offers, with the hope she can market her work for pay. What EWS realizes is that if education is needed to develop a person in every aspect of life,[63] then widows like Hassana are underdeveloped. Consequently, their human capacities to effect social change are limited.[64] Ruth, a widow I introduce fully in chapter 5, received formal education, and acquired marketable skills at EWS.[65] Because of her education and marketable skills, Ruth was hired to teach at EWS. Therefore, she is contributing to the cognitive development of other widows.

Ruth is also able to use her education and acquired skills to manage her small farm. She bragged that even people in the community rave about her farming skills. Ruth shares some of what she grows to help other people. She even gives some of the proceeds from her crops to EWS. What she gives goes into what EWS spends to house the widows, feed the widows, and maintain the school. Ruth joins the cohort of benefactors who also pay part of the widows' tuition and give them material goods (i.e., clothes, raw food, and lotions) to nurture and educate their children. What Ruth's story underscores is that when widows' economic needs are met, they express economic agency that leads to social change. Most importantly, what inspires widows like Ruth to contribute to the economic empowerment of other widows is their faith in God. I recall Ruth's words: *Idan Allah ya albarkache ni, ba sai in albarkache wani ba?* ("If God blesses me, should I not bless another person?") As I already demonstrate, this sentiment is behind the economic agency of other widows, too. To continue exploring the agency of Christian widows in northern Nigeria, I discuss their social agency by showing the ways widows exercise their social agency within society.

Social Agency of Christian Widows

In his book *Exclusion and Embrace*, Miroslav Volf argues that exclusion of people who are alien or different is among the most intractable problems in

---

62. Ladi Musa, interview by author, April 19, 2017.
63. Okoye, *Widowhood*, 166.
64. Okoye, *Widowhood*, 169.
65. Ruth, interview by author, April 25, 2017.

the world today.[66] Volf praises the inclusive narratives of every society; however, he cautions that those same narratives often exclude certain groups who disturb the integrity of society's "perfect" plots. Volf posits that if the healing word of the gospel is to be heard today, Christian theology needs to discover avenues of speaking that address the hatred of the other. Volf reaches back to the New Testament metaphor of salvation as reconciliation by proposing the idea of embrace as a theological response to the problem of exclusion. Volf reveals that exclusion is our primary sin because it distorts our views of reality and causes us to react out of apprehension and anger to anyone who is not within our ever-narrowing circle. In view of this, Volf states that Christians should learn that salvation involves being reconciled to God, learning to live with others, and opening ourselves to the other by embracing them in the way that God embraces us. Unfortunately, widows have limited access to social resources to enhance their social agency. Most importantly, their limited presence within society deprives them of the social resources necessary to effect social change. However, the widows' faith demands their participation in African social life.

The Role of Faith in the Social Agency of Christian Widows

Note that Volf challenges Christian agency based on biblical principles. In other words, he grounds social agency on faith when he challenges Christians to address social issues by emulating God. It is almost the same thing that the contributing authors of *Development and Politics from Below* do. Their position also buttresses the position I cited earlier in this study, which states that Africans would reject social change that weakens their religious convictions. In a way, Volf is making the same appeal by asking, "Does embracing the other weaken your religious order?" What Volf and the contributors of *Development and Politics from Below* suggest is that if a Christian widow refuses to embrace others, her faith in God needs to be reexamined. This is because faith is pertinent towards social agency in Africa.

Noting the complex shifts between politics, religion, and development in Africa, the contributors of *Development and Politics from Below* strongly counteract the modernist and secularist positions, which suggest that religion would become irrelevant and therefore should be ignored. The contributors of the book realized that religion in Africa is a decisive factor in both politics and development. The contributors capture this dynamism by

---

66. Volf, *Exclusion and Embrace*.

moving beyond confined ideas of politics and development and private and public spaces to understand modern notions of religion in Africa. Their aim is to understand how religion is embedded in the lives of Africans who are struggling to survive and make sense of the world. In a sense, the book demonstrates that the widows' social engagement is an embodiment of their faith. Thus, religion finds expression through social engagement in northern Nigeria.

To discuss the role faith plays in the ways Christian widows in northern Nigeria can participate in social change, I will use Dorothea E. Schulz's article, "Remaking Society from Within: Extraversion and the Social Forms of Female Muslim Activism in Urban Mali" as a springboard.[67] In the article, Schulz examines female Muslim activism by underscoring the role Muslim women's religious sociality plays in remaking society from within. The article emphasizes the socially constructive influence of Muslim women's activities as they seek to engage contemporary debates about political Islam from a different viewpoint; this includes political Islam's new public representations and significant dangers and the apparently new roles and yearnings that religious movements claim in modern African politics. Schulz situates this current movement historically to convey the social thrust of this activism; that is, its current capacity to attract and express the moral consternation of a broad range of followers. Schulz states that:

> As structures of sociability, learning and mutual support, women's "religious" associations allow them to claim collective relevance at the interstices of domestic, semi-public settings, and to initiate new nodes of articulation between society and the state. As such, female Muslim activism in Mali is a particular modality of "politics from below," one that aims not at a political protest but at the transformation of the personal and the social.[68]

This is significant to my position in this study because Schulz asserts that faith motivates the social agency of women. In other words, faith makes women's contributions relevant to the socio-political realities of Africans. The widows I interviewed protest political structures by pointing out the decadence of the political process. They are confident that they can effect social change by transforming the socio-political structures. What makes them confident that they can effect change is that God enables them to do so. Evelyn, a widow, said, "If God does not change Nigeria, no one can

67. Schulz, "Remaking Society," 74.
68. Schulz, "Remaking Society," 89.

change Nigeria."[69] It is this deep-seated spiritual conviction that motivates widows' social agency in northern Nigeria. Allow me to unpack the significance of that conviction as it pertains to widows' social agency that leads to social change.

Schulz introduces the idea of women groups that coalesce around a common vision of social change. While Schulz recognizes some of the challenges of women groups (i.e., the hierarchical nature of the groups that undermines the issue of equality), she endorses women groups that aim to transform society from within. A veteran widow, Gimbiya, admonished the young widows to "collect yourselves in prayer groups, so you can have accountability and strengthen each other."[70] Note that prayer informs widows' social agency in northern Nigeria. What this means is that widow support groups engender a theologizing that helps widows address societal needs. The women groups at GAWON and EWS provide avenue for theologizing widows' lives within northern Nigeria. With prayer as a foundation, widows are challenged to resist societal demands that undermine their social agency.

Oduyoye also advocates for women groups, in this case, "Christian women," because such groups help the widow gain inclusivity and give the widow a better representational voice in society.[71] In other words, what widows' groups provide for the widow is a place for inclusion and a "voice" for the widow so that the widow provides inclusion and voice to others in society. This is what I draw from Volf, who admonishes Christians to embrace others just as Christ has embraced and engendered their agency. The widows' groups become places where the widow is embraced to help her process betrayal and hurt as she learns to embrace others.

Towards Inclusivity

The widows' stories underscore their marginality. The marginalization of African women is based upon theories of exclusion.[72] In northern Nigeria, a widow is expected to live in isolation from society upon her husband's death. In fact, widowhood dons a veil of silence. But how can Christian widows in northern Nigeria heal the breaches within their community if they are forced to operate in exclusive structures? Volf's book, which

---

69. Evelyn, interview by author, April 13, 2017.
70. Gimbiya, interview by author, March 29, 2017.
71. Oduyoye, *Daughters of Anowa*, 130.
72. Schulz, "Remaking Society," 198.

largely addresses enmity created by civil wars, is applicable in the ways that African cultures treat widows. His argument suggests that the war against widowhood in African societies needs to be resolved, and African societies need to find ways to learn to live with the widow.

When Joyce became a widow, she felt the sting of loneliness that is exacerbated by the stigma associated with widowhood. One stigma is that widows are considered perpetual "beggars." Because people assume widows always need money, Joyce said whenever family and friends see her, they would start complaining about their own economic struggles before hearing what she had to say.[73] This is to discourage Joyce from asking them for any favors. What Joyce's family and friends do not realize is that their attitude towards her further marginalizes her. In fact, Joyce said the treatment she has received from them caused her to feel *banza* ("worthless"). Those words reveal the heart of a widow whose social agency is impacted by a warped perception of what people think of her. Joyce's situation underscores the need for widow's groups that give her a sense of inclusion. These groups would strengthen her faith, so she could navigate the challenges of widowhood and discover how to use her divine status to effect social change.

In identifying the impact women groups can make in transforming society, Schulz highlights the focus of development theorists and practitioners on social arrangements. Social arrangement has to do with the way society is structured to engender interactions between people. Social arrangements have especially been the focus for most of the proposals on the problem of exclusion in any context. What Schulz demonstrates is that social arrangements are inevitable within society. Social arrangement forms the basis of Volf's concept of the "other." The concept of the "other" suggests there are people who exist within structures that isolate them. Widows in northern Nigeria exist within those types of structures. Since we cannot deny social arrangements, what Volf suggests is that Christians transform social arrangements that isolate widows like Joyce by embracing her. In other words, there is need to reform the existing social structures in northern Nigeria to include widows in the conversation towards social change.

However, African women also need to demand inclusion that pushes the conversation further on social change. Enid Schildkrout indicates that women would embrace social arrangements that engender their agency.[74] But Dorothea Schulz suggests that women embrace social arrangements

---

73. Joyce, interview by author, March 16, 2017.
74. Schildkrout, "Widows in Hausa Society," 151.

Agents of Social Change

that empower them to transform society.[75] This is what Schulz means when she states the importance of faith in personal and social transformation. This is also at the core of Volf's contention that Christians should follow their convictions towards agency that results in social change. Christian convictions focus on the transformation of the personal and the social. Because they are driven by Christian spirituality, EWS and GAWON provide avenues for personal and social transformation of widows. Consequently, the widows' groups at EWS and GAWON already provide a template for enabling widows to contribute towards each other's transformation. At EWS, because the widows live on campus, they encourage each other. As articulated in the opening story of this chapter, the veteran widows mentor the young widows, offering them counsel on how to live as widows. This also takes place at GAWON, where older widows also mentor young widows when they gather for their monthly meetings. The cooperative groups, led by widows, create a forum for the widows to share their stories and for veteran widows to share their wisdom with the young widows.

The widows at both organizations become *kishiyan juna* ("each other's friend"). They recognize that reforming structures that marginalize them demands solidarity. Standing as individuals allows oppression to readily weigh widows down. The solidarity between widows engenders agency. Therefore, widow groups enhance the social agency of Christian widows. The sense of inclusion widows find among the group of other widows positions them to become agents of social change. Specifically, inclusivity within these groups positions widows to become voices for the voiceless in society.

Towards a Representational Voice

Mercy Oduyoye asserts that the priorities of African women begin and end in relationships.[76] Oduyoye describes this relationship thus:

> African women have supported each other through, networks of kindred, friends, wives of an affinal home, women selling the same commodity, or women passing on skills of pottery, weaving or beadwork. Whether it was birth, marriage or funeral, African women got together and worked. Women supported women, standing in solidarity with women.[77]

---

75. Schulz, "Remaking Society," 199.
76. Oduyoye, *Daughters of Anowa*, 131.
77. Oduyoye, *Daughters of Anowa*, 198.

Oduyoye's description above contributes to numerous conversations regarding the role of women as peacemakers in Africa.[78] Upon recovering their own voices within the embracing community of other women, the widows become voices for others' liberation. A widow named Tani embodies this vision. Tani and her husband had five children. As a policeman in northern Nigeria, her husband's salary was meager. She was faithful to him. But when he got promoted at his job, he became abusive towards her. Unbeknownst to her, he married another woman. She also found out that he had impregnated several other women. Things got worse when he lost his job. Instead of looking for another job, he frequented bars and brothels. Tani was neglected. When she became pregnant, he did not care for her. Very soon, he became deranged. He often slept on the side of the road. He became very sick. It was later discovered that he had acute ulcers, which caused him to bleed uncontrollably. She spent the very little she had to nurse him while taking care of herself and her children, including her unborn child.

When her husband died, she took the burden of caring for her children. Today, she has successfully raised the children alone. Society was complicit in her struggle because no one gave her a voice amid her turmoil. The isolation that is characteristic of widowhood prevented her from participating in support groups until she came to EWS. Buoyed by her faith, she attends EWS with a vision: "My ambition is to mentor widows, and they would teach others [widows]. This is how Nigeria would be transformed."[79] For Tani, her experiences and biblical training have given her a platform to transform the lives of others. Tani is only one of several widows who realized that their empowerment is incomplete if they fail to empower other widows. She believes that the best teacher for a widow is another widow because the widow comprehends the plight of another widow.

Two implications come to mind when widows are given a voice. First, Dorothea Schulz notes that while "Muslim women" groups do not usually originate for political reasons,[80] they influence secular politics.[81] This is equally true of widows in northern Nigeria who either run for office or adopt a political candidate to support during elections. Even when their

---

78. Zaggi, "Nigeria"; Biddle, "Women as Peacemakers"; Wundengba, "Role of the 21st-Century Woman"; Ogoloma and Ukpere, "Role of Women in Peacemaking"; Garba, "Building Women's Capacity," 31–46.

79. Tani, interview by author, March 16, 2017.

80. Schulz, "Remaking Society," 77.

81. Schulz, "Remaking Society," 78.

candidacy or candidate does not win, their aim is always to use their political platform to give voice to many marginalized groups in the country. And second, just as the Muslim women groups that Schulz discusses see themselves as moral agents within their communities, so do Christian widows' groups in northern Nigeria. For instance, Christian widows' groups aim to rid society of its evils through piety. Volf would describe the socio-political agency of widows as an imposition of truth that offers gains in power.[82] He states that this goes against traditional philosophers who have struggled to use truth to gain knowledge rather than power.[83] And this is not to say that every widow is using biblical truth to gain power; in fact, the axiom that "knowledge is power" applies to Christian widows in northern Nigeria. It is the reason why this study considers education pertinent towards the agency of widows.

Therefore, Christian widows need biblical truth that gives them the power towards social agency, where they empower other widows and marginalized groups within society. Widows need power that positions them to effect social change. As they live in solidarity with each other, they keep issues of marginalization in the public spaces.[84] In other words, the widows take the truth across every social boundary.[85] The widows become moral agents as they give voice to everyone in society. Thus, through solidarity to each other widows are empowered towards agency. What undergirds widows' social agency is their faith in God. Faith ensures greater effectiveness as moral agents. It is faith that motivates widows to use their limited roles to help other widows and other marginalized groups within society.

To conclude, faith ensures that Christian widows contribute to greater religious, economic, and social achievements of northern Nigeria. I noted that the widows consider God as their "helper." Such a belief is borne out of gratitude and trust in God. Christian widows trust God to help them draw from the lessons of their widowhood to effect social change. Therefore, the widows express gratitude because God helps them to effect greater economic, religious, and social agency towards social change.

---

82. Volf, *Exclusion and Embrace*, 248.
83. Volf, *Exclusion and Embrace*, 248.
84. Oduyoye, "Widows and African Rituals," 199.
85. Oduyoye, "Widows and African Rituals," 199.

Religious, Economic, and Social Agency

Doing a Lot with Little: How Faith Engenders Greater Achievements

What is evident from my description of the agency of Christian widows is that widows have very little religious, economic, and social resources to make significant impact. In other words, structures of exploitation and impoverishment have rendered widows economically, socially, and spiritually poor. Faith engenders widows' agency because faith undergirds their lives. What I mean is they recognize that the best way to overcome structures that marginalize them is a resilient faith in God. Such a faith transforms widowhood into a period of calling. Christian widows believe God uses their widowhood experiences to call them to agency that leads to social change.

In their widowhood, God helps the widows to critically reflect on the relevance of their faith to identify the structures of exploitation and impoverishment against their struggle towards agency. All my respondents believed that widowhood trains the widow to do a lot with little. Thus, widowhood prepares widows to use meager economic, social, and religious resources towards significant social change. Bonat succeeded in raising godly children and transforming society with meager resources. She had little biblical training, little finances, and little relationships to enable her to raise godly children that are transforming society. Hajara and Ruth also had little religious, economic, and social resources to contribute significantly towards social change.

My point is that widows' agency arises from limited religious, economic, and social resources that are characteristic of widowhood. What this means is that their agency comes from a place of poverty that leaves room for God to enrich their widowhood towards social change. Thus, widows contribute significantly to the religious, economic, and social realities of northern Nigeria because God magnifies their little resources towards greater social change.

Conclusion

Widows consider widowhood a divine charge towards agency; they believe that God accords them the status necessary to effect significant social change in their roles as wives and mothers. Therefore, I argued in this chapter that faith engenders greater religious, economic, and social agency towards social change. And what becomes apparent in discussing the agency of Christian widows is that widows' agency arises from limited religious, economic, and social resources that are characteristic of widowhood. In other words, faith motivates greater religious, economic, and social achievements that lead to social change in northern Nigeria. Theological issues become vital towards empowering Christian widows to become agents of social change in northern Nigeria. Therefore, Christian institutions have the grave responsibility of guiding widows' agency.

4

Christian Institutions and Agency
A Study of African Pentecostalism

INA OMAKWU HAD AN evangelistic zeal. As a child from southern Nigeria, Ina grew up under the careful supervision of his parents who instilled their Christian faith in him. Throughout his life and ministry, he focused on what he believed God had called him to do. In 1993, Ina and his wife, Sarah, established a church called *Family Worship Center* in Abuja, Nigeria. They started with about two hundred people in attendance. Presently, the church has about fourteen thousand people in attendance every Sunday.

The Family Worship Center, hereafter FWC, is part of newer Pentecostalism that combines strong biblical faith and advocacy. FWC's motto is "The people who care." This motto is expressed in the church's diverse ministries, which include discipleship training school, care groups, ministry of help, and visitation ministry. Of importance to this study is the church's Missions Department, which focuses on helping widows. Since becoming the church's sole leader upon Ina's death in 2003, Sarah has boosted the ministry to widows. The church increased its economic, social, and spiritual support to widows. Particularly, FWC provides housing for the widows and their children and secures employment for the widows. And the church provides guidance for the widows on ways to invest money, raise their children, and grow deeper in faith.

FWC exemplifies the holistic approach to ministry that is congruent with the African worldview of these widows. When I asked the widows to tell me what institutions guide the agency of Christian widows in northern

Nigeria, several widows said, "Family Worship Center." I share the stories of three of those widows in this chapter. One of them, Jummai, describes what FWC does for widows:

> They give us monthly stipends. They pay our children's school fees. We are invited to attend a conference for both spiritual and physical support. We meet with other widows and participate in worship. They conduct prayer and healing services for us. During the meeting, we are provided legal assistance. The church invites lawyers and judges to the event to provide free legal consultation. I enjoyed the teaching for widows to stand on their feet and face their challenges.[1]

Jummai brimmed with joy as she narrated what FWC does for widows. In addition to what Jummai states FWC does to empower widows, FWC also collects photos of the widows and their children to pray for them and rally support on their behalf throughout the year. FWC also communicates with the widows regularly through phone calls and texts. It is important to note that Jummai is the principal of EWS, but she sees FWC as an exemplar for holistic approach to development.

In this chapter, I argue that Christian institutions best guide the agency of Christian widows in northern Nigeria. I describe the social institutions in northern Nigeria as I show the pertinent role Christianity plays in guiding widows' agency. In doing so, I provide a brief historical background on how Christian institutions became central to development initiatives in Africa. Then, I examine how Pentecostalism in its institutional form best guides the agency of people in northern Nigeria. Finally, I suggest two pertinent ways that Pentecostalism effectively guides the agency of widows in northern Nigeria.

Social Institutions in Northern Nigeria

Social institutions, hereafter "institutions," are a central area of study within the social sciences. A typical definition of institutions within the social sciences is that proffered by Jonathan Turner:

> A complex of positions, roles, norms, and values lodged in particular types of social structures and organizing relatively stable patterns of human activity with respect to fundamental

---

1. Jummai, interview by author, March 24, 2017.

problems in producing life-sustaining resources, in reproducing individuals, and in sustaining viable societal structures within a given environment.[2]

Several descriptions of institutions have elements of Turner's definition. For instance, Anthony Giddens states that "institutions by definition are the more enduring features of social life."[3] Political scientist Samuel Huntington further describes institutions as "stable, valued, recurring patterns of behavior."[4] As mechanisms of social order, institutions dominate the behavior of people in every society. Institutions are guided by a social objective, which transcends individual aims by moderating the dictates that govern living behavior.[5] There are more descriptions of institutions I could provide. But what every description of institutions underscores is that institutions are pertinent to the life of any society. In other words, any society that takes the development of its people seriously ensures that it has strong institutions.

The major institutions in northern Nigeria are family,[6] politics,[7] economics,[8] healthcare,[9] education,[10] and, most importantly, religion.[11] Religion is the most important institution in northern Nigeria because other institutions are subservient to the religious institution. What I mean is that because religion undergirds the lives of people in northern Nigeria, religious sentiments guide their interactions with institutions. Gregg Okesson expresses concern about the collusion between institutions and religious sentiments. In an article, "Christian Witness to Institutions," Okesson explores witness to institutions by addressing the issue of power through sociological, theological, and missiological lenses.[12] Okesson states that when institutions assume powers that aid people to define reality and, in some instances, become related to supreme meaning, this can either lead to complicity where religious capital can sacralize the public domain or entreat

2. Turner, *Institutional Order*, 6.
3. Giddens, *Constitution of Society*, 24.
4. Huntington, *Political Order*, 9.
5. Stanford Encyclopedia of Philosophy, "Social Institutions."
6. Macionis and Gerber, *Sociology*, 116.
7. Connor, "A Nation Is a Nation," 377–400.
8. Denhart and Jeffress, "Social Learning," 113–25.
9. Institute of Medicine, *Insuring America's Health*.
10. United Nations, "1966 International Covenant."
11. Vaidyanathan, "Religious Resources?" 366–87.
12. Okesson, "Christian Witness," 142–54.

society from religious domain to pursue independence or immortality.[13] This is a legitimate concern.

However, my research shows collusion is already taking place between institutions and religious capital because Nigerians view everything through the prism of faith. The widows are not convinced that safeguarding institutions from religious domain can help engender their agency. What their responses demonstrate is that "Christian institutions"[14] best guide the agency of Christian widows in northern Nigeria. The impact of Christian institutions in the lives of widows in northern Nigeria was evident in the responses I received from the widows when I asked them to tell me what institutions best guide their agency. At EWS, 70 percent of the widows mentioned schools and churches; 20 percent mentioned government; 20 percent mentioned hospitals; 20 percent mentioned NGOs; and 10 percent mentioned banks. At GAWON, 70 percent mentioned NGOs; 30 percent mentioned churches; 20 percent mentioned support groups.

The responses reveal three pertinent things. First, the widows highly rated the institutions (i.e., EWS and GAWON) they currently belong to as vital to guiding their agency. In other words, widows at EWS consider schools valuable to guiding their agency, while widows at GAWON consider NGOs valuable to guiding their agency. Second, government appears as a separate institution from anything else on the list. In other words, the widows did not refer to schools, hospitals, support groups, and banks managed by government. The Nigerian government operates several institutions that include hospitals, schools, and banks. However, government institutions

---

13. Okesson, "Christian Witness," 145.

14. Based on my premise that the other institutions the widows listed are subservient to the (mainline) church, I use the expression "Christian institutions" to refer to churches, schools, hospitals, NGOs, support groups, and even banks that are influenced by the church. Influenced by mission agencies that birth them, mainline churches compete with the government by establishing churches, schools, and hospitals, and they also inspire the establishment of NGOs, support groups, and financial aid centers around the country. ECWA, the denomination that most of these widows belong to, manages schools, hospitals/clinics, and a bank. In fact, it is conventional knowledge in Nigeria that the most effective institutions are those established or associated with the church. There will be instances where it is necessary to refer to the "church" in isolation from the other institutions; however, I want to underscore the far-reaching influence of the church even when referred to in isolation from the other institutions associated with the church. And this is not only limited to Protestant churches. Catholic churches have always been engaged in establishing and managing schools and hospitals, for instance. Regarding hospitals, it is estimated that faith-based organizations provide between 30–70 percent of health care services in Africa (USAID, "The Key Role of Faith-Based Organizations").

have failed to meet people's social needs.¹⁵ Azza Karam suggests that the reason government institutions fail to meet people's needs is because the religious dimension is missing.¹⁶ By that, Karam means that government institutions resist subservience to religion. The significance of religion in African development has resulted in churches playing significant roles in development in northern Nigeria.¹⁷ Therefore, the institutions the widows mentioned above are influenced or managed by Christian principles. I provide a brief historical background to how Christian institutions assumed a prominent place in African development shortly.

And third, the cumulative responses from the widows at EWS and GAWON gave churches the highest mention overall (50 percent). NGOs came in second (45 percent), then schools (35 percent), then government, support groups, and hospitals (10 percent each), and banks (5 percent). Widows at EWS ranked churches (70 percent) equally with schools (70 percent) as the preeminent institutions that best guide their agency. This is not surprising, since EWS is managed by a church (ECWA). On the other hand, the widows at GAWON ranked churches (30 percent) as institutions that best guide their agency; however, they ranked NGOs highest (70 percent) as the institution that best guides their agency. It is also not surprising, since GAWON is an NGO. However, there is a caveat to that ranking. The widows at GAWON do not think of GAWON in isolation to the church; in fact, the reason they ranked GAWON highly is because Christian principles guide its operations. Christian spirituality is the most pertinent social capital of institutions in the rural contexts of northern Nigeria. The historical backgrounds of most, if not all, institutions in the rural settings of Kaduna are based on Christian spirituality.

Because of the pertinent role of the church towards agency, there is need to further describe the role of religion to development within Africa. Here, I provide a brief historical background of how Christian institutions assumed a prominent place in African development. My aim is to demonstrate that Christian institutions best guide the agency of Christian widows because Christianity promotes a holistic approach to development. As I noted in the introduction of this study, a holistic approach to development is an important theme of embodiment. I show the beginnings of the ways a

---

15. Myers, *Walking with the Poor.*
16. Karam, "Role of Religious Actors," 367.
17. Gifford, *African Christianity*, 22–26.

holistic approach to development is used to engender the agency of Christian widows in northern Nigeria.

The Church and Development in Africa: A Brief History

There was optimism amidst the euphoria when many African states, such as Nigeria, became independent in the 1960s. The indigenous leaders of these African states commenced implementing strategies towards modernization; however, lacking appropriate local models, they used Western models (i.e., rational-legal) that soon failed them. This failure plunged African states back to patrimonialism,[18] where people at the lower end of the totem pole became "retainers whose position depends on a leader to whom they owe allegiance."[19] Paul Gifford notes that "corruption" and "clientelism" are manifestations of Africa's modern patrimonial systems.[20] African leaders modeled their authority on the Western rational-legal model while operating on a patron-client system. Gifford asserts that it is this "dysfunctional neo-patrimonial political culture that is primarily responsible for Africa's present plight."[21] My objection to Gifford's statement is his use of the word "dysfunctional." Gifford insinuates, perhaps without realizing it, that there is some redemptive aspect of neo-patrimonialism. Patrimonialism is itself a dysfunction that contributes to the present plight of Africa.

And I know Gifford would agree that patrimonialism is itself a dysfunction, since he suggests that the only hope Africa has of joining the modern world is to outstrip neo-patrimonialism, administer the rule of law, construct institutions, and "adopt rational bureaucratic structures, systems, and procedures in education, health, agriculture, transport and so on."[22] And I must say that the one effective institution that Africans have built is the church, especially since the church exerts significant influence

---

18. Some might even argue that African states never departed from patrimonialism but attempt to erect Western institutions on top of patron-client foundations. This is a legitimate point.

19. Gifford, *African Christianity*, 5.

20. Gifford, *African Christianity*, 5. Corruption refers to officials who exercise their powers not as a form of public service but of private property. Clientelism, on the other hand, is a relationship of exchange between a patron and a client, a relationship whereby an elite provides security for an inferior citizen and the citizen provides political support to the elite.

21. Gifford, *African Christianity*, 10.

22. Gifford, *African Christianity*, 11.

on the other structures, systems, and procedures Gifford refers to. Simply, the church assumed a prominent place in the development efforts in Africa.

Even sociologists point to the pertinent place of the church in development. For instance, Emile Durkheim defined religion as a "unified system of beliefs and practices relative to sacred things."[23] By sacred things, Durkheim means things "set apart and forbidden—beliefs and practices which unite into one single moral community called a Church, all those who adhere to them."[24] Durkheim's definition readily associates religion to the institutional church because he recognizes not only the prominent place of religion but specifically the prominent role that Christian institutions play within human society.

What makes Christian institutions most effective in guiding the agency of widows is that they have a holistic approach to development within northern Nigeria. What I mean is that Christianity engenders a holistic approach to development by linking the theological and the social realities of life. No wonder Fatima depends on Christian institutions for her spiritual and physical needs because "sustainable development is impossible without religion."[25] For Christian widows in northern Nigeria who see their material circumstances through the prism of religion, they expect the church to help them use their faith to control the forces of their lives.[26] Widows recognize that Christian approaches to development are based on a holistic framework where their material and spiritual needs are met.

Stephen T. Ellis and Gerrie Ter Haar provide a broad perspective of how religion engenders a holistic approach to development within Africa. Drawing from anthropologist Edward Tylor, Ellis and Ter Haar define religion as "belief in the existence of an invisible world often thought to be inhabited by spirits that are believed to affect people's lives in the material world."[27] First, the definition affirms that many people in the world are religious.[28] This is certainly true of widows in northern Nigeria. Christian sentiments undergird every aspect of their lives. Second, the definition incorporates practices often considered "superstition," which is meant to

---

23. Durkheim, *Elementary Forms*.
24. Durkheim, *Elementary Form*.
25. Ellis, "Development," 24.
26. Ellis, "Development," 25.
27. Ellis and Ter Haar, *Worlds of Power*, 3; Tylor, *Religion in Primitive Culture*, 8.
28. Ellis and Ter Haar, *Worlds of Power*, 3.

exclude other religious forms.[29] The holistic framework of northern Nigeria makes it impossible to exclude other religious forms in guiding the agency of Christian widows towards agency. What this refers to is the point in chapter 2 that Christianity draws from ATR and even Islam in northern Nigeria towards guiding agency.

Third, the definition includes both "constructive" and "destructive" practices.[30] As I have suggested, Christianity in northern Nigeria can enhance positive and negative social changes. And, finally, the holistic vision of religion in Africa requires a break from the Western proclivity to define religion almost exclusively as a search for meaning in life.[31] What Ellis and Ter Haar advocate is a robust understanding of the ways religion engenders a holistic approach to development that best guides the agency of Christian widows in northern Nigeria.

My respondents underscore the fact that Christian institutions engender a holistic approach to development in guiding the agency of Christian widows. It is therefore not surprising that my respondents placed the heaviest responsibility on Christian institutions for guiding the agency of Christian widows in northern Nigeria. Takai Shamang also believes that Christian institutions should bear the responsibility of helping widows in northern Nigeria.[32] And Ladi Musa's narrative about EWS's inception reveals the important role Christian institutions have continued to play in guiding the agency of widows at EWS.[33] And despite her statement that churches do less to help widows, Donna Pridham believes that Christian institutions best guide the widows' agency in northern Nigeria.[34]

One of the ways Christian institutions best guide the agency of Christian widows is through education. Mercy's husband died and left her with six children. She secured a bank loan to start a restaurant business. While she runs the business, she attends EWS. So it was not surprising that she listed banks and schools in her response to my inquiry on institutions that guide widows' agency. However, she credits her successes to EWS for "equipping me to be what I am today."[35] Mercy's statement reflects the senti-

29. Ellis and Ter Haar, *Worlds of Power*, 3.
30. Ellis and Ter Haar, *Worlds of Power*, 3.
31. Ellis and Ter Haar, *Worlds of Power*, 3.
32. Takai A. Shamang, interview by author, March 27, 2017.
33. Ladi Musa, interview by author, April 19, 2017.
34. Donna Pridham, interview by author, March 24, 2017.
35. Mercy, interview by author, March 16, 2017.

ments of every widow on the significant role Christian institutions play in their lives. The word "equip" refers to her experiences at EWS, which means she believes EWS is preparing her to fulfill her calling as a widow in northern Nigeria. Like most widows, Mercy could have chosen to go anywhere, but she chose to attend EWS because the biblical training would help her know how God wants to use her situation to transform society.

Education: How Biblical Literacy Engenders Agency

EWS has taught widows how to read and write throughout its history. EWS recognizes that a holistic approach to development involves training widows' minds. I suggest in this study that appropriation has to do with how widows draw upon Western and African motifs to meet societal needs. Education ensures that widows can wisely draw from those motifs to effect positive change. Particularly, biblical literacy is pertinent towards the ever-expanding agency of widows in northern Nigeria.

Therefore, the purpose of learning to read and write is to read the Bible. When I asked several widows in a literacy class at EWS how learning to read and write might boost their agency, Naomi, a veteran widow, said, "It will enable us to read the Bible to know what God expects of us."[36] The other widows nodded approvingly. What Naomi's response suggests is that biblical literacy is pertinent towards guiding their agency. Or, to put it another way, biblical literacy helps widows to know how their faith engenders their agency. The strong relationship between biblical literacy and agency underscores the fact that Christian institutions have a pertinent role towards guiding the agency of Christian widows. Christian institutions best guide Naomi's ambition to become a teacher by continuing to provide sound biblical instruction. Naomi wants to teach children to inculcate in them a spiritual vigor she believes is necessary towards positioning them to contribute positively to society. She believes a biblical-centered training at EWS is foundational to her ambition to pursue a teaching certificate. By guiding her agency, Christian institutions ensure widows like Naomi are positioned to effect social change.

---

36. Naomi, interview by author, April 13, 2017.

Agents of Social Change

A Major Shortcoming of Christian Institutions

However, given the correlation between biblical literacy and agency, I am concerned that the model for educating widows at EWS has residues of colonial Christianity that undermine the ways Christian institutions guide the agency of Christian widows. By "colonial Christianity," I am referring to imported Christianity from the West. These residues of colonial Christianity tend to elevate Western models of education over African models. EWS's literacy classes utilize textbooks and workbooks written by Westerners. The biblical literacy program at EWS uses a Western model of rote learning, which focuses on short-term recall.[37] I found the widows in a literacy class memorizing portions of a textbook in preparation for an exam. While rote learning has its merits, care must be taken to ensure that it does not overshadow behavioral learning models, which focus on helping widows based on their perceived needs. Because ECWA has not shrugged off this aspect of colonial Christianity, the curriculum EWS provides for training widows is largely based on a Western model of rote learning.[38]

Therefore, even the biblical instruction tends to draw more from Western models by using more cognitive approaches and less from African models which require engaging the behavioral aspects of widows. Cheryl Pridham, a Westerner, also laments the fact that the curriculum used at EWS draws from Western models.[39] She recognizes the need for ECWA to take the behavioral aspects of widows into account as EWS guides them towards agency. What Pridham's lament suggests is that neglecting the behavioral aspects of widows can be detrimental in guiding their agency. Christian institutions have the responsibility of guiding the agency of Christian widows by providing biblical instruction that draws upon Western and African motifs that lead to social change.

Drawing from Western models and neglecting African models undermines the holistic approach to the development of Christian widows towards agency. Colonial Christianity's shift to a more dualistic expression of faith due to the influence of hard science also meant a shift away from biblical Christianity. One of the areas one sees the influence of dualism is the waning of biblical instruction in mainline churches. Thus, contemporary mainline churches have succumbed to a dualism that undermines biblical

---

37. Ong, *Orality and Literacy*.
38. Cheryl Pridham, interview by author, March 24, 2017.
39. Cheryl Pridham, interview by author, March 24, 2017.

truth. However, R. Horton notes that some Nigerians resist the dualistic approach towards ministry by forming their own kind of Christianities.[40] Christian widows in northern Nigeria are gravitating to these newer forms of Christianities because these newer churches, *inter alia*, emphasize a holistic approach to development. In other words, these churches are committed to guiding the agency of widows based solely on biblical principles. And these types of Christianities do not only hold the Bible in high regard but promote the idea that the Bible can help people control the forces of their lives and effect social change. Thus, using cognitive and behavioral models of learning,[41] these churches implement diverse teaching elements to assist widows to "receive, process, remember, and replicate news, important information, and truths" that leads towards social change.[42]

In northern Nigeria, African Pentecostalism at its institutional nature effectively guides the agency of widows by providing a holistic approach to development that enables widows to appropriate Western and African motifs towards agency.[43] I unpack some aspects of African Pentecostalism, hereafter "Pentecostalism," to demonstrate the ways Pentecostalism as an institution best guides the agency of women. Fundamental to the effectiveness of Pentecostalism's efforts in guiding the agency of widows are two aspects of Pentecostalism: the core of its theology and where it draws its theological cues. These two undergirding aspects of Pentecostalism inform my description of the ways Christian institutions best guide the agency of Christian widows in northern Nigeria.

Pentecostal Theology and the Widows' Agency

The first aspect of Pentecostalism is what the core of its theology is. It is impossible to provide a robust account of Pentecostal theology here; therefore, I state some of the essential tenets of Pentecostalism to move the discussion forward. Pentecostalism is a renewal movement within Protestant

40. Horton, "African Conversion," 85–108.
41. Leach, "Orality and Learning Theories."
42. Madinger, "Literate's Guide," 15. Madinger describes the concept of orality and its implications for the theory and practice of missions around the globe.
43. The term "Pentecostalism" has a variety of meanings. Gifford, *Ghana's New Christianity*, refers to them as "faith gospel" and "new churches." Meyer, "Going and Making Public," uses "Pentecostalism" and "prosperity gospel" interchangeably. Other authors prefer the more controversial expression "Pentecostal-Charismatic." Clearly, they are distinguished from the African Initiated Churches (AICs).

Christianity that places special emphasis on a direct personal experience of God through baptism with the Holy Spirit.[44] The Holy Spirit is the most common feature of Pentecostalism in northern Nigeria. The role of the Holy Spirit is evident in Pentecostal beliefs on divine healing, which requires faith in Jesus as the Healer; the imminent return of Christ, which explains the urgency of evangelism within Pentecostalism; spiritual gifts, which is largely evident through speaking-in-tongues; and a triune God.[45]

The Holy Spirit is at the core of Pentecostal theology. I demonstrate the role of the Holy Spirit when I discuss the specific ways Pentecostalism guides the agency of Christian widows. Meanwhile, what I want to state is that the core of Pentecostal theology is the Bible. The Bible is the basis for how Pentecostalism guides widows' agency. Richard Burgess notes, "African Pentecostals look for correspondences between their own life circumstances and the Bible. They expect Biblical texts to have practical relevance and problem-solving potential through the mediation of the Holy Spirit."[46] What this means is that Pentecostalism's understanding of the role of the Holy Spirit in guiding the agency is based on biblical principles. Based on the Bible, Pentecostalism holds that the presence of the Holy Spirit leads to a vigorous and daring faith that brings happiness, health, and prosperity in every aspect of life.[47] The Bible helps widows discern how the indwelling Holy Spirit engenders their agency towards social change.

It is not necessarily that the widows endorse Pentecostal theology since they maintain their memberships at their mainline churches. But they are attracted to how Pentecostal institutions guide the agency of their

---

44. This is called being "born again," a fundamental requirement of Pentecostalism where one is said to fully experience the power of God in every aspect of life.

45. These beliefs apply to most of global Pentecostalism. However, it is important to point out a major area of disparity within Pentecostalism. The trinity is where this division is more pronounced. While most Pentecostals believe in the orthodox doctrine of the Trinity, as one God in three persons (Father, Son, and Holy Spirit), Oneness Pentecostals (apostolic Pentecostals/Jesus-only Pentecostals) are non-trinitarian, believing in one divine Spirit who reveals himself in several ways. This position emerged in opposition to newer Pentecostalism in 1914, a few years removed from the Azusa Revival. While there are many Oneness Pentecostals, they pale in comparison to the Trinitarian Pentecostals. Obviously, there are other areas where Pentecostals differ on doctrine and practice, but they are not as pronounced on the issue of the Trinity. Furthermore, these differences are influenced by the contexts in which Pentecostalism is practiced.

46. Burgess, "Pentecostals," 196. See also Kalu, *African Pentecostalism*.

47. Gifford, *Ghana's New Christianity*.

Christian Institutions and Agency

adherents through strong biblical admonition.[48] Every widow that receives assistance from FWC is drawn by its biblically driven theology that feeds into their everyday lived realities. Jummai noted: "Through FWC teaching widows to stand on their feet, I gained a lot."[49] She underscored how the biblical teaching she received at FWC is helping her discern the ways the Holy Spirit is guiding her agency. For this reason, Jummai exercised her agency that leads to social change by providing leadership at EWS.

My point is that Pentecostalism considers the Bible the most important symbol for guiding the agency of Christian widows towards social change. This is not to say that mainline churches do not recognize the importance of the Bible. But, as I show, biblical instruction is waning in mainline churches. The Bible is pertinent in shaping the brighter future widows anticipate for themselves and for society. The Bible is a powerful symbol because it legitimizes new and better realities by redeeming the widowhood ritual. Because of the powerful symbol of the Bible within Pentecostalism, widows receive guidance on how to embody the ways mourning rituals lead to social change. Thus, Pentecostalism sees widowhood as a phase where widows continue to have God-given capacity towards agency. For this reason, Pentecostalism best guides the agency of Christian widows.

The second aspect has to do with where Pentecostalism takes its theological cues. In his book *African Pentecostalism*, Ogbu Kalu demonstrates the astonishing diversity of African Pentecostalism that thrives in several forms within diverse local contexts.[50] He argues that African Pentecostalism is characteristically African. According to Kalu, African Pentecostal theology draws heavily from African indigenous religions.[51] Allan Anderson, a foremost scholar on global Pentecostalism, concurs with Kalu that African Pentecostal theology takes it cues from the indigenous religions.[52] Anderson demonstrates that one of the ways African Pentecostalism draws from the indigenous religions is by using traditional views of witchcraft, for instance, to articulate its theology of power.[53] This is an example of "appropriation." Charmaine Pereira and Jibrin Ibrahim note that Pentecostalism is a salient social movement that articulates and appropriates new

48. Deborah Bonat, interview by author, March 24, 2017.
49. Jummai, interview by author, March 24, 2017.
50. Kalu, *African Pentecostalism*.
51. Kalu, *African Pentecostalism*, 181.
52. Anderson, "African Indigenous Churches," 197–98.
53. Anderson, "African Pentecostal Churches."

configurations of power in practical ways to mediate Nigerians' current needs.[54] In other words, Pentecostalism guides widows on the ways to draw upon Western and African motifs to change society.

Kalu and Anderson's positions suggest the idea of appropriation because African indigenous religions involve Western religious motifs. Recognizing this, Pentecostalism tends to keep both motifs, affirming more of the African motifs. What this allows is for Pentecostal adherents to appropriate Western and African motifs towards effecting social change. Because Pentecostalism as an institution is engaged in appropriation, widows that are connected to Pentecostal churches such as FWC are appropriating Western and African motifs toward social change. This appropriation ensures that widows formulate transformative theologies for themselves and others.

Before I venture into articulating the specific ways Pentecostal theology best guides the agency of widows for social change, I want to discuss positive and negative contributions of Pentecostalism in guiding agency in northern Nigeria. My aim is to show how Pentecostalism's biblically driven theology that draws upon Western and African motifs can negatively or positively impact the agency of widows. This is important to this study because effecting change must consider the ways that measures have been successful or have failed to provide proper guidance towards social change. This ensures that whatever strategies are formulated mitigate or avoid the failures that inhibit widows' agency towards social change.

The Negative and Positive Contributions of Pentecostalism to Agency

In her book *Political Spiritualities*, Ruth Marshall discusses what led to the rise of Pentecostalism and how it influences the social and political dimensions of life.[55] Marshall attempts an interdisciplinary approach to examine how Pentecostalism presents the experience of being born again as a way for Nigerians to realize the promises of political and religious salvation made during the colonial and postcolonial eras. Marshall's analysis of this religious trend highlights Nigeria's contemporary politics, postcolonial statecraft, and the everyday struggles of ordinary citizens coping with poverty, corruption, and inequality. Marshall surmises that Pentecostalism is a global phenomenon, as she suggests that Nigeria is an important case

54. Pereira and Ibrahim, "On the Bodies of Women," 925.
55. Marshall, *Political Spiritualities*.

study that demands thinking about the place of religion in modern politics. Marshall notes that Pentecostalism constitutes the single most important socio-cultural force in Nigeria today.[56] What Marshall means is that Pentecostalism is central to the lives of people in Nigeria. Given the importance of Pentecostalism in Nigeria, Marshall discusses the negative and positive contributions of Pentecostalism in guiding agency within Nigeria. Because there are several positive and negative contributions of Pentecostalism, I highlight one positive and one negative contribution that are relevant to the ways Pentecostalism guides agency in northern Nigeria.

The Negative Contributions of Pentecostalism to Agency in Northern Nigeria

Marshall admits that Pentecostalism has played a decisive role in increasing political division and violence along religious lines.[57] That Pentecostalism has been a polarizing phenomenon in Nigeria is not surprising, since Pentecostalism engages the public. Recounting the origins and characteristics of Pentecostal-Charismatic movements in northern Nigeria, Matthew A. Ojo articulates the tension that Pentecostal zeal creates between Christians and Muslims.[58] He argues that Muslims respond to the evangelistic zeal of Pentecostals in northern Nigeria with violence, a reality that Ojo calls "the formidable barrier to Christian missions."[59] I do not think this is intentional on the part of Pentecostalism, but the confrontational nature by which Pentecostal theology is expressed makes it the most unfavorable Christian expression to Muslims in northern Nigeria. Therefore, Pentecostalism can engender Christian widows to contribute to socio-political dissent that leads to violence.

Further, Pentecostal zeal that promotes violence is linked to the prosperity gospel that is pervasive among Pentecostal churches in Nigeria.[60] Gifford states that prosperity gospel is irreconcilable with effective economic ventures because it advances patrimonialism and deflects attention from the structural roots of poverty.[61] Such a reality makes marginalized

---

56. Marshall, *Political Spiritualities*, 2; see also Mustapha, "Ethnicity," 257–75.
57. Marshall, *Political Spiritualities*, 2.
58. Ojo, "Growth of Charismatic Movements," 88.
59. Ojo, "Growth of Charismatic Movements," 88.
60. Burgess, *Nigeria's Christian Revolution*.
61. Gifford, *Ghana's New Christianity*.

groups subservient to the elite within the social structure. What I mean is that patrons such as Pentecostal pastors can recruit marginalized groups such as widows to participate in dubious acts for remuneration. Although no evidence exists of Pentecostal pastors recruiting people to engage in violent behaviors, the prosperity gospel has the potential of endorsing violent aggression towards others by promoting a link between Christian maturity and material wealth. Thus, rather than embodying social change, widows become nuisances to the society they are called to change. Consequently, the widows fail to be agents of social change; rather, they promote violent repercussions for society.

The Positive Contributions of Pentecostalism to Agency in Northern Nigeria

Pentecostalism has progressive views about women in the public sphere. What undergirds Pentecostalism's progressive views towards women is the indwelling Holy Spirit. Such progressive views broaden widows' access to economic, social, and religious resources. By that, I mean Pentecostalism emphasizes people's capacity to broaden access to jobs, contracts, and welfare facilities.[62] A broadened access to resources provides Christian widows in northern Nigeria a path towards their long-term goal of using their God-given status to effect social change. Simply, Pentecostalism enables widows to determine their lives in freedom.

Rebecca Ganusah admits that while Christianity has sometimes been a factor for violence in Africa, the role of Christian institutions in Africa is pertinent to the development within Africa.[63] And despite the political divide and violence caused by the enthusiasm of Pentecostal churches in northern Nigeria, some authors show that widows in northern Nigeria have found these Pentecostal churches salient to their lives.[64] In his article "Max Weber Is Alive and Well, and Living in Guatemala," Peter Berger states that Pentecostalism is the best thing that happened to developing countries.[65] Berger also notes that Pentecostalism's stress on motivation, entrepreneurship, and discipline is the Protestant work ethic. David Martin argues that

62. Pereira and Ibrahim, "On the Bodies of Women," 926.
63. Ganusah, "Church and Development," 203–18.
64. Brusco, *Reformation of Machismo*.
65. Berger, "Max Weber Is Alive and Well," 3–9.

African Pentecostalism leads towards modernity.[66] And Matthew Ojo also notes the modernizing tendencies of Pentecostalism.[67] What these authors echo is Marshall's sentiment that Pentecostalism occupies a central place in the lives of people in Nigeria. Most importantly, Pentecostalism guides the agency of Christian widows by broadening their access to resources that position them to effect social change.

In sum, Pentecostalism contributes both negatively and positively to agency in northern Nigeria. Pentecostal zeal can engender violent aggression towards others, which undermines the gospel. Nevertheless, Pentecostalism is an important social force that best guides agency. But given the fact that Pentecostalism contributes negatively towards agency means, like other Christian institutions, Pentecostalism is also "broken." Here, I hearken to Gregg Okesson's suggestion that the solution to broken institutions is not to demonize them, but to witness to them.[68] Okesson states that institutional power often coheres to a social imaginary that dwells deep within a person's soul.[69] What Okesson recognizes is that Christian institutions will always influence the lived realities of people in Africa. But the aim of such witness is that Christian institutions will use their power *wisely* in guiding the agency of Christian widows.

And when Christian institutions use their power wisely to guide the agency of Christian widows, they help widows to become agents of social change. And such effectiveness must never understate the ability of local people to choose from the array of Western and African motifs to meet societal needs. Perhaps what makes FWC effective in guiding widows' agency is that it combines Western and African motifs. By that, I mean the FWC's ministry to widows uses cognitive and behavioral methods to guide widows on ways to meet the specific needs of their communities. Jummai said what she receives from FWC enables her to provide leadership to the widows at EWS.[70] She has watched several widows graduate from EWS, ready to use what she and others have invested in the widows to help them become agents of social change in northern Nigeria.

The ability and freedom to appropriate different religious expressions of faith provide the widows with diverse resources to effect social change.

66. Martin, *Pentecostalism*, 152.
67. Ojo, "Growth of Charismatic Movements," 91.
68. Okesson, "Christian Witness," 142–54.
69. Okesson, "Christian Witness," 145.
70. Jummai, interview by author, March 24, 2017.

In other words, the ability and freedom to appropriate their faith sets the widows on the path towards a victorious future. Because widowhood depicts a life of despair, widows embrace the reality of a victorious future for themselves and for society. Thus, Pentecostalism helps widows to see widowhood as a vehicle towards agency.

Towards a "Victorious" Future

In *Christianity, Development and Modernity*, Paul Gifford devotes an entire chapter to the theme of victory, demonstrating that development leads to a glorious destiny.[71] Widows like Jummai anticipate this glorious destiny. In fact, I found that *nasara* ("victory") is an important word for the widows in northern Nigeria. They described the type of future they want as a "victorious" future. Theresa Adamu's first book on widowhood deals with how a Christian widow can be victorious.[72] I also perused autobiographical books written by widows that emphasized the ways to be victorious as a widow. For instance, Comfort Janfa describes her life as a widow with a title that includes the word "success."[73] Jummai said the widows are taught that seeking God leads to victory.[74] Fatima summarizes it well: "The primary aim of life is for the widows to be victorious."[75]

Even though widows from mainline churches desire a victorious future, Christian institutions fail to address their needs in a way that leads to that victorious future. The problem has to do with not taking the behavioral aspects of widows into account. In other words, Christian institutions attempt to address widows' needs by drawing from Western motifs and neglecting African motifs. Moreover, the theology of these Christian institutions rarely includes the word "victory." I am not suggesting that Pentecostals have a monopoly of the word "victory," but Pentecostal theology is replete with it. And this theology influences Christian widows from mainline Protestant and even Catholic traditions. The widows believe Pentecostalism best guides their agency because it ensures the victorious future they seek for themselves.[76]

71. Gifford, *Christianity, Development and Modernity*, 29–44.
72. Adamu, *Nasarar Gwanruwa Kirista* [*The Victory of a Christian Widow*].
73. Janfa, *Mystery of Success*.
74. Jummai, interview by author, March 24, 2017.
75. Fatima, interview by author, March 27, 2017.
76. I use the terms "Pentecostalism" / "Pentecostals" / "Pentecostal churches" to show

Furthermore, Richard Burgess notes that Pentecostalism's focus on social change is a vital spiritual element that motivates Pentecostals to engage the public space.[77] In other words, the victorious future Pentecostalism promises is not just for its adherents, but for society. Thus, Pentecostalism enables its adherents to engage the public space from a victorious posture. I observed that the widows who seemed more autonomous despite the challenges of widowhood were those connected to FWC. Simply, they engage the public space from a victorious posture. By that, I mean they interact with people based on what they can give others rather than on what they can receive from others. They are not dependent on others; others depend on them (i.e., children, in-laws, and widows).

There are two pertinent areas in which Pentecostalism best guides the agency of people that other Christian institutions might emulate: *a heightened spirituality* and *a hierarchical leadership*. What these two areas demonstrate is the role that the Holy Spirit plays in engendering the agency of Christian widows in northern Nigeria, with the Bible as the foundation. Specifically, the Holy Spirit empowers widows to become agents of social change in northern Nigeria.

Heightened Spirituality

I use the expression "heightened spirituality" because the widows talked about the fact that Christian institutions help them "to add to their knowledge of God." Their goal is to be spiritually revitalized for the future they anticipate. A heightened spirituality does not mean that widows want to overspiritualize everything, but it bespeaks the abiding presence of the Holy Spirit who helps widows to be agents of social change. Matthew Ojo states that Pentecostals are striving to renew the Christian faith by restoring whatever spiritual vitality has been lost in the existing churches.[78] David Martin asserts that Pentecostals are prompted by the New Testament where they are challenged to recover those aspects of the gospel that they believe is lost in a mainline rationalized Christianity, especially the gifts

---

how the movement guides the agency of widows. However, the terms also include the institutions established, managed, and/or influenced by Pentecostalism. I chose not to use the term "Christian institutions" to refer to Pentecostal institutions to ensure a clear distinction from mainline churches.

77. Burgess, "Pentecostals," 195.

78. Ojo, "Growth of Charismatic Movements," 91.

of Pentecost.[79] In short, Pentecostals aim to recover the New Testament, especially Luke-Acts, and their account of the origins of the church when the Holy Spirit fell upon the disciples. The rallying call of Pentecostalism is that all Christians possess spiritual gifts and thus have power for agency.[80] Although Gifford cites this rallying call of Pentecostalism as a weakness because pastors function as "spiritual specialists," Pentecostalism insists that the Holy Spirit is pertinent towards guiding the agency of widows. In short, widows cannot add to their knowledge of God or be spiritually revitalized for the future without the Holy Spirit.

Asabe's husband was sick until his death. He left her with several children to raise. But, unlike most widows, she spoke less about her children. It was not that she did not care for her children. I was just struck that after listening to the other widows speak vociferously about their children, she said very little about them. Rather, she narrated an event that happened before her husband's death. After one of his bouts with ill health, Asabe said God woke her up one night to inform her of her husband's imminent death.[81] After his death, her in-laws confiscated her property and maltreated her. When she shared her dream with someone at FWC, they encouraged her to purchase a piece of land. She used her savings to do so. I was struck that a widow from a mainline church says she hears from God. For a widow to speak about hearing from God is "scandalous" within the mainline church where Asabe is a member. As far as her church is concerned, if society is not allowed to interact with her, then God is not allowed to interact with her either. Her life is supposed to be that of alienation and isolation even from God. However, FWC affirmed her claims about hearing from God. As of the time we met, FWC continues to guide her agency. In fact, Asabe said FWC is the only institution that she knows of that guides the agency of widows.

Asabe's connection with FWC has given her renewed spiritual vigor. FWC affirmed her spiritual gifts, which is the recognition that she has power to effect social change. Birgit Meyer attributes Asabe's spiritual vitality to Pentecostal pastors who contribute to organizing a distinct, new religious public that advocates a born-again personal identity and recasts society as a site of a spiritual battle between God and Satan.[82] Pentecostalism assures Asabe that God erases the boundary lines that perpetuate her suppression.

79. Martin, "Pentecostalism," 38.
80. Ojo, "Growth of Charismatic Movements," 91.
81. Asabe, interview by author, March 28, 2017.
82. Meyer, "Going and Making Public," 157–58.

Christian Institutions and Agency

This explains why Asabe said, "If you dedicate your life to the Lord, you will overcome."

What Asabe's statement underscores is that Pentecostalism does not only guide her agency towards personal spiritual vigor, but Pentecostalism guides her agency towards the spiritual vigor of others within society. Marshall notes that conversion is more complex than simply following Jesus; it involves a break from the past and venturing into a perpetual state of uncompromising existence.[83] In other words, by breaking from the past, widows enter the perpetual state of becoming agents of social change in the power of the Holy Spirit. Asabe told me FWC has encouraged her to pursue her calling to be a missionary.[84] As I listened to Asabe, I could not help but think of Eileen Lageer's words about how womanhood that is emancipated and elevated through the preaching of the gospel can be invaluable to the church.[85] In fact, Asabe states: "widowhood can be a path towards spreading the gospel." But widowhood can be such a path when Christian institutions provide the guidance widows need towards agency.

In her role as spiritual mentor to other widows at EWS, Asabe encourages widows to pursue their own callings towards social change. She assures them that "God hears the widow." Of course, this is the experience that was vital towards her deeper understanding of God. Given the challenging social, economic, and even religious atmosphere in northern Nigeria, Asabe motivates widows to embrace the type of vibrant spirituality Pentecostalism accords its adherents towards agency. What Asabe demonstrates is that Pentecostalism provides a platform for widows to participate in creating new and better realities in northern Nigeria.

Because Pentecostalism reclaims the agency of the Holy Spirit on all Christians, Pentecostalism best guides widows' agency by promoting their spiritual vitality. Pentecostalism accomplishes this by affirming widows' spiritual gifts and encouraging them to pursue their calling towards agency. Doing so positions widows to wield more influence within society. Due to the agency of the Holy Spirit, a heightened spirituality enables widows to assume consequential positions within society.

---

83. Marshall, *Political Spiritualities*, 131.
84. The mainline church Asabe belongs to reserves such a role only to a man.
85. Lageer, *New Life for All*, 78–79.

Agents of Social Change

Hierarchical Leadership

Pentecostalism also best guides widows' agency by how it affirms widows' spiritual gifts, which encourages them to pursue their calling through the agency of the Holy Spirit. The term "hierarchical" needs some clarification. I understand that mainline churches are largely hierarchical. However, by using the term here, I am suggesting that Pentecostalism allows women to assume positions of authority within society. Pentecostal churches have hierarchy too, but it has more fluidity. In other words, the hierarchy within Pentecostal churches avoids much of the dogma of mainline churches, where movement up and down the leadership ladder happens in one direction. Marshall cites that Pentecostal pastors describe their "call" as coming from a personal revelation through a personal communication with God. This is either affirmed by others or resisted. This is because, according to Marshall, even classical, bureaucratic Pentecostal churches tend to determine leadership based solely on the directive of the Holy Spirit.[86] By that account, this allows every Pentecostal, including women, to embrace their callings that are legitimated by Pentecostal churches.

However, Gifford is right that the emphasis on the Holy Spirit can also sanction patron-client relationships in the churches. There are two grave dangers to pastors who function as "spiritual specialists" and as patrons. The first danger is that these pastors assume a place equivalent to God. For this reason, their actions are never or hardly scrutinized. They can wield their power for their own benefit. The second danger is that these pastors tend to exchange spiritual services for material gains. Widows, who lack material resources, are neglected. Therefore, my description is based on Christian institutions that use religion wisely to guide the agency of widows. By that, I assume that these institutions hearken to the directive of the Holy Spirit to guide widows to be agents of social change.

In her article "Arise, Oh Ye Daughters of Faith," Damaris Parsitau suggests that Pentecostalism gives its adherents access to the Holy Spirit, and the Kenyans she interviewed are empowered by that promise.[87] What this underscores is that spiritual gifts, not gender, qualify people to be agents of social change. That Pentecostalism places theological importance on one's calling accounts for the multiplicity of female roles in Pentecostal movements. Parsitau's argument points out that this is a significant shift from the

---

86. Marshall, *Political Spiritualities*, 133.
87. Parsitau, "Arise."

Christian Institutions and Agency

ideology of mainline Christianity. It suggests that Pentecostalism heralds a novel phase that has remarkably affected the status of women, especially single, divorced, and widowed women. In fact, Parsitau asserts that single, divorced, and widowed women have assumed leadership roles within society.[88] For instance, some of these women are vital to the founding, expansion, and sustenance of churches. It is significant that all female-led churches in Africa are Pentecostal churches, although some older African Instituted Churches (AICs) were headed by women. These "pre-Pentecostal churches," as Kalu calls AICs, were known as "spirit-empowered movements" that either arose independently of or out of Western mission churches.[89] This is not surprising, since these churches have continued to guide women's agency.

Parsitau admits that the role of women in Pentecostalism is still a contentious issue; however, she states that because of the nature of Pentecostalism, women have made progress in challenging patriarchy in the church and public culture. Thus, the "born-again" reality leads to revaluing oneself in relation to God and others. In Pentecostalism, the Holy Spirit helps widows to move from victimhood to an active engagement with their circumstances, from dependence on politicians to the cultivation of transnational networks.[90] In short, widows are encouraged to overcome evangelical gender stereotypes by being agentic. This has inspired widows such as Asabe to participate in the public sphere of northern Nigerian society. And such agency is enhanced by the ways FWC guides her agency in northern Nigeria. Because of the active involvement of Pentecostals in the public space, widows associated with Pentecostalism are involved in the public space as they contribute significantly to addressing developmental challenges in society.

Women assuming more active roles within society have huge implications. I have already related that Jummai uses the instructions she received from FWC to lead the widows at EWS. Sarah, the third widow to receive support from FWC, shares a similar story with Jummai. Sarah's husband died six years before our meeting and left her with four young daughters.[91] Despite her desire to pursue an education and to educate her daughters, she lacked economic, social, and religious resources. This is when FWC

---

88. Parsitau, "Arise," 131.
89. Wariboko, "Pentecostalism in Africa."
90. Parsitau, "Arise," 143.
91. Sarah, interview by author, March 24, 2017.

came in. They provided the resources Sarah needed towards autonomy and agency. Due to FWC's guidance, Sarah completed her degree and was the vice principal of EWS at the time of our meeting, which pays her enough to educate her daughters and even support other relatives. She aims to reproduce the type of guidance she received from FWS to the widows she is mentoring. Like Jummai, Sarah has mentored several widows by helping them become agents of social change.

Pentecostalism enables widows to overcome structures that have limited their agency within society. Sarah makes it clear that FWC gives women the chance of a career and adventure they are denied in society, which involves taking a stand against a corrupt world.[92] This is reminiscent of my conversation in chapter 3 about women groups being moral agents within society. However, while some mainline churches aim to guide the agency of widows, the widows continue to be inhibited by a rigidity that undermines the role of Christian institutions in guiding the agency of widows. By "rigidity," I mean the inability to recognize the dynamic nature of the Holy Spirit in guiding agency as Pentecostalism recognizes.

Therefore, Christian institutions need to convert to the ways the Holy Spirit engenders agency. I concur with Okesson that witnessing to institutions must start inside the church.[93] Okesson argues that for Christians to witness to institutions, they must be transformed by that same witness first.[94] Such witness is pertinent because structural power is often unaware of the people's real needs. Decisionmakers are usually disconnected from the people. Thus, churches establish institutions in local communities to serve the needs of the people; however, those needs continue to go unmet because those institutions tend to focus on perceived needs rather than the actual needs of the people. What is needed is for Christian institutions to have the freedom to fully understand the needs of widows to guide their agency. There is a need to humanize Christian institutions, and by that I mean creating and maintaining institutions that serve people rather than power structures. When that happens, Christian institutions best guide widows in northern Nigeria towards a victorious future for the widow and for society.

In sum, Pentecostalism best guides the agency of widows through a heightened spirituality and hierarchical leadership for widows. These

---

92. Gifford, *Christianity, Development and Modernity*, 72.
93. Okesson, "Christian Witness," 151.
94. Okesson, "Christian Witness," 151.

pertinent areas are based on Pentecostalism's biblical understanding of the agency of the Holy Spirit in the lives of Christian widows. Thus, Pentecostalism's emphasis on biblical faith aligns with the widows' convictions that a spiritually grounded faith is a necessary guide towards their agency. And the ambitions of most widows are for Christian institutions to guide them towards greater spiritual vigor and for the widows to use their spiritual gifts to transform society. This ambition is in tandem with the fact that the presence of the Holy Spirit opens all the "publics" of society to the widow.

Conclusion

Christian institutions best guide the agency of widows that leads to social change. Christian institutions are central to development initiatives in Africa because the Bible promotes a holistic vision of development. Specifically, biblical literacy is pertinent towards helping widows draw upon Western and African motifs to effect social change. Pentecostalism best guides the agency of widows because the Bible is central to Pentecostal theology. Although Pentecostalism guides people to contribute negatively to society, it also significantly guides people to contribute positively to society. Because its biblically centered approach underscores the agency of the Holy Spirit in the lives of every believer, Pentecostalism guides widows to a victorious future through heightened spirituality and hierarchical leadership. The next chapter lays a theoretical framework, demonstrating a theological development of an embodied agency that leads to social change.

5

A Theological Proposal for Embodied Agency

CHRISTIAN HISTORY SHOWS THAT communities developed new areas for theological development at the intersections of culture and faith. I suggest that contemporary times require new ways of theologizing about embodiment in Africa. Theological development of embodiment involves the process of appropriating Western and African motifs in northern Nigeria. Aided by the Christian resources that help them appropriate diverse motifs, Christian widows are theologically trying to make sense of what is going on in their lives through embodiment. This chapter describes how Christian widows can do more to embody the ways mourning rituals will lead to social change in northern Nigeria. I will be using "embodiment" to refer to the widows' physical bodies and how their bodies can mediate the transforming power of Jesus' incarnation within society.

In previous chapters, I attempted to reveal fresh theological undertakings happening within social and religious realities on the agency of widows. My goal here is to build on this framework, providing fresh alternatives for locating embodiment in Jesus' incarnation because Christian widows are inspired by the life of Jesus in the power of the Holy Spirit. Thus, Jesus' incarnation is the model for how widows can embody the ways mourning rituals will lead to social change. Consequently, I sought for authors that articulate a strong link between incarnation and embodiment. Ola Sigurdson's work on incarnation and embodiment provides the clearest

A Theological Proposal for Embodied Agency

link between incarnation and embodiment.[1] Sigurdson's description of the interaction between incarnation and embodiment exposes the deficiency in the Christology of the African male theologians I state below.[2] What I mean is that Sigurdson's work not only provides a more comprehensive description of incarnation and embodiment but shows the clearest links between them. Therefore, I find his work most relevant to my framing of a theology of embodiment. However, given that I am using a non-African/Africanist theologian to frame my argument, it is important to consider my reasons for doing so by examining some key African Christological works.

African Christology

African theology is rich in Christology. Through a Christological lens, salient works by African theologians such as Bolaji Idowu,[3] Jean-Marc Ela,[4] Ogbu Kalu,[5] John Mbiti,[6] and Kwesi Dickson[7] analyzed and interpreted the relationship between African traditional religion and global Christianity. Kwame Bediako,[8] Lamin Sanneh,[9] and Agbonkhianmeghe Orobator[10] ar-

---

1. One other work that also aims to link embodiment and incarnation is *The Power of Interpretation*, edited by Klaus Hock. Unfortunately, the book was impossible to access as of the time of compiling this study. The inaccessibility of the book is quite disappointing because the reviewers I read suggested two articles in the book, "This Is My Body" and "Christian Identities and Development in Northern Nigeria"; these articles might have helped me to further develop my framework. Based on the reviews I read, Hock and the contributing editors examine novel structures of Christian life in Africa and pertinent factors that shape them. The editors conclude that these new structures must be interpreted by considering the influence of new interpretive orders that stem from complex arrangements where new structures of Christian life within Africa are formulated into a new vision for Africa, where essentialism and dichotomy are out of bounds.

2. Sigurdson's philosophical analysis of the incarnation is quite robust. In a Google search for "Incarnation and Embodiment in Africa," Sigurdson's book came second. The first was an article by Jakub Urbaniak titled "Between the Christ of Deep Incarnation and the African Jesus of Tinyiko Maluleke." Urbaniak's article means that Sigurdson's work is the most comprehensive on the link between incarnation and embodiment.

3. Idowu, *African Traditional Religion*.
4. Ela, *African Cry*; Ela, *My Faith as an African*.
5. Kalu, *African Pentecostalism*.
6. Mbiti, *African Religions and Philosophy*.
7. Dickson and Ellingworth, *Biblical Revelation and African Beliefs*.
8. Bediako, *Christianity in Africa*.
9. Sanneh, *Translating the Message*.
10. Orobator, *Theology Brewed in an African Pot*.

gued for the importance of translating the gospel into African contexts. Also, Bediako and John Pobee[11] developed an African Christology based on the ancestors. Contemporary Nigerian theologians are also engaging in the Christological debates within Africa. Specifically, Yusufu Turaki[12] and Jacob Olupona[13] are two of a plethora of Nigerian scholars whose works engage the Christological implications for Nigerians. Others are Afe Adogame and Matthews Ojo, whose contributions are highlighted in this study. Most of these theologians are among the seventy scholars that contributed to the *Africa Bible Commentary*.[14] The commentary reveals how African evangelicals are wrestling with developing a Christian theology that is contextually African. Thus, African evangelicals are developing Christian theologies that speak to the issues Africans face. These theologians have provided fodder for theological conversations around the world. Their perspectives continue to shape the theological landscape.

However, their rich Christology fails to adequately engage the issue of women's embodiment through the lens of the incarnation of Jesus for two reasons. First, the evangelicalism that these African authors embody can be said to be "American and conservative." By that, I mean the Christology of many of these African male theologians is influenced by the works of several American theologians.[15] Moreover, they are largely selective of Western theologians they consider conservative in their approach to the Bible.[16] Even African theologians recognize the influence of conservative

---

11. Pobee, *Toward an African Theology*.
12. Turaki, *Tainted Legacy*.
13. Olupona, *African Traditional Religions*.
14. Adeyemo, *Africa Bible Commentary*.
15. I use the word "most" because I concede that not all of them pander to their Western counterparts. Orabator's book *Theology Brewed in an African Pot* (2008) easily comes to mind. In this book, Orabator provides a fascinating preamble to Christian theology from an African perspective. What is unique about the book is that Orabator uses parts of Chinua Achebe's well-known novel *Things Fall Apart* (1958) to explore key themes in Christian theology. Having said that, Orabator also elucidates the distinctions between African and Western views of religion. This buttresses my point that African theologians write in response to their Western counterparts.
16. A case in point is Archbishop Peter Akinola, the former Anglican Primate of the Church in Nigeria. Akinola is known for opposing theological developments he believes are incompatible with Scriptures and orthodox Anglicanism. He is notably known for opposing same-sex blessings and any homosexual endorsement within the church. But Akinola's theological approach is not strictly African, given his international network.

American theology within their own Christology.[17] Second, African male theologians abide by the "distance" that African culture demands between men and women. Therefore, they write in vagaries regarding women's experiences because they do not fully understand the lives of women, especially widows. Even if they write on women, their views are based largely on conventional thoughts about widowhood, for instance. They fail to examine the widow's lived realities to assess her unique needs. Therefore, their works do not provide the clearest links between embodiment and incarnation as it pertains to widows.

Women's embodiment has been left to feminist theologians. Feminist theologians such as Mercy Amba Oduyoye, Fulata Moyo, Musimbi Kanyoro, and Isabel Phiri articulate a Christology that takes seriously the experiences of African women. Unfortunately, most of their works speak in generalities of women's experiences, thereby giving little attention to the specific plights of African widows.[18] Nevertheless, I draw upon feminist theologians to propose a theology of embodiment through the lens of Jesus' incarnation. Thus, despite their limited attention to the specific plights of African widows, feminist theologians provide some link between embodiment and incarnation that is invaluable to this study. Moreover, feminist theology provides some background to the lives of widows that is lacking in Sigurdson's work.

My goal in this chapter is to locate the embodiment of mourning rituals in the Spirit of Jesus towards social change. Because widows are theologically trying to make sense of what is going on in their lives through embodiment, I argue that widows can embody the ways mourning rituals will lead to social change by mediating the power of Jesus' incarnation. Integrating the previous chapters, I propose a theology of embodiment that demonstrates what Christian widows could do with agency. I weave a conversation between Sigurdson and feminist theologians to show the link between embodiment and incarnation that engenders social change.[19] Then, I show

---

17. Kato, *Theological Pitfalls*, 60.

18. African widows get little to no attention from the literature. The ethnography in Betty Potash's volume (*Widows in African Societies*) provides unique experiences of widows in Africa; however, it is purely an anthropological approach. Kirwen (*African Widows*) draws from the incarnation in his descriptions of widows in East Africa; however, the incarnation is not the framework on which he bases his arguments on African widows. I cite these books in this study.

19. I should note that radical feminism considers religion antithetical to the liberation of women. In fact, it rejects the notion of Jesus as an exemplar for women's liberation.

that widows are using Christianity and social change, holistic approaches to development, and inculturation to embody the ways mourning rituals will lead to social change by mediating the power of Jesus' incarnation.

Before I venture further, let me expound on the theme of "gaze" because it links embodiment and incarnation in this study. Couched between his conversation on the incarnation and embodiment, Sigurdson discusses the concept of gaze.[20] Sigurdson examines the way cultural and historical factors impact the way we see the world around us. He suggests that what links gaze and the world people inhabit is the understanding that humans are embodied beings.[21] The concept of gaze is pertinent to this study because the embodied agency of Christian widows suggests "seeing" them and acknowledging they have pertinent roles to play toward social change. For Christian widows in northern Nigeria, gaze highlights the need for an embodied agency that mediates the power of Jesus' incarnation towards social change.

After interviewing some staff members at GAWON one afternoon, an administrator asked me to give one of the widows a ride to a nearby hospital for her weekly health consultations and to collect antiretroviral medications, since she was HIV positive. It was a quiet ten-minute drive to the hospital. She was modestly dressed: white blouse, colorful wrapper, bangles, necklace, shoes, and earrings. This struck me because veteran widows hardly dress up the way she did. And this is because widows are expected to live in a perpetually grief-stricken state. However, this widow's appearance defied that. It seemed like she was going to a ceremony, and not to a hospital.

I forgot about the uneventful drive to the hospital that day until an interview I had with another widow, Ruth, who was also HIV positive.[22] Ruth grew up in a rural town in northern Nigeria. She got married in her mid-teens. She was a faithful wife and mother. But Ruth endured physical

---

However, reformed feminists provide a less extreme approach. They refuse to be as overfixated on Jesus' maleness as radical feminists; rather, they focus on the implications of Jesus' humanity to the liberation of Africa's women. It is this reformed feminist view that I will draw upon in this study.

20. The term "gaze" consists of a wide-ranging undertones and disciplines. I choose not to limit myself to one connotation or discipline here, although my use of the term is highly influenced by art history. Marita Sturken and Lisa Cartwright provide a more succinct account of the term from diverse perspectives in *Practices of Looking*.

21. Sigurdson, *Heavenly Bodies*, 151–293.

22. Ruth, interview by author, April 25, 2017.

and emotional abuses from her husband. Her in-laws also abused her. When her husband found out he had contracted HIV due to his infidelities, he refused to tell Ruth. And he convinced the doctor not to tell Ruth of his HIV status. As a result, he transmitted the virus to Ruth. When he became extremely sick, Ruth nursed him until his death. Soon, she got sick, too. She consulted a different doctor who confirmed that she was HIV positive. Unable to keep the secret, she informed her family, including her in-laws. She did not only faced further marginalization but lost custody of her two older children and was left to cater for her young children. Her financial, health, and marriage statuses made it especially difficult for her to take care of her children. Finding a decent job that paid enough for her to take care of her children was impossible. Male benefactors pretended to help her, only for her to realize their intentions were to sleep with her. She was even bold enough to tell one of them she was HIV positive, risking further marginalization. When she refused to "repay" them with sex, they required repayment of the help they provided her with interest; otherwise, they threatened to spread rumors that she was prostituting herself to take care of her children. Apart from further marginalization, those rumors could be grounds for losing her young children. But Ruth overcame the odds. Today, she teaches at EWS, where she uses her body to mediate her story of redemption and hope to inspire widows to embody the ways mourning rituals can lead to social change in northern Nigeria.

Ruth's story took me back to the uneventful drive with that widow whose body revealed scars from the wounds of neglect, betrayal, abuse, and injustice. I noticed that during our drive, she kept looking at her body. She only raised her head to notify me that we were close to the hospital. Using her right index finger, she stroked her left hand by drawing imaginary lines on her arm. It was as if she was mapping her story with those imaginary lines. During our interview sessions, I also noticed that most of the widows gazed at their bodies a lot. While this is not unique to widows, it was particularly poignant given what they have been through. Like the widow I drove to the hospital, they touched their bodies when they spoke to me. I also observed this trend during chapel services, class sessions, group sessions, cooking lessons, and walks to the market. My conversation with Sabina indicates that touching their bodies is part of the process of getting to know their bodies towards an embodied agency. At fifty-four years old, Sabina has experienced it all. She became a widow at twenty-five years old when her husband was killed by Boko Haram militants. She remarried, but the man died after a brief illness. After his death, she focused on raising her four children. Successfully raising them to become independent, Sabina enrolled at EWS. When I asked her why she decided to come to school, she responded, "Though I was old, I wanted to know what is in my body. Understanding what was in my body would help me in the situation I found myself."[23] And she believes her embodiment is part of her religious realities by crediting her experiences to God's will: *Duk abin da ya faru da ni, Allah ne ya yarda* ("All the things that happened to me, God allowed it"). By crediting her experiences to God's will, Sabina believes it is God's plan to prepare her to embody the mourning rituals that will lead to social change. Thus, EWS uses Christian principles to guide Sabina, which, according to Sabina, enables her to mediate "God's grace within society."

That Ruth and Sabina mediate the grace of God demonstrates that the incarnation influences their embodied agency. I propose the biblical concept of "incarnation" because the widows showed extraordinary hope in Jesus as they embraced their callings to embody the ways mourning rituals will lead to social change. Sabina articulated this hope when she spoke about how Jesus informed her of her husband's death: "When my husband was about to die, Jesus woke me up to inform me of his imminent death." She said that Jesus literally touched her to awaken her. She said, "I will never forget that experience because it helped me to know Jesus is with me." Given the marginalization associated with widowhood, Sabina's statement is quite poignant. The statement does not only suggest that God is present with her in her widowhood, but it also suggests that the incarnation is a pertinent motif for how Sabina can embody the ways mourning rituals will lead to social change. Thus, Jesus' incarnation engenders her embodied agency. As Samira, a young widow, said: "Jesus helps me to live out the word of God."[24]

Sigurdson on Embodiment

In his book *Heavenly Bodies*, Sigurdson argues that Christianity does not scorn the body but affirms human embodiment.[25] He offers his contribution to historical and modern conceptions of the body by exploring anthropological implications of the doctrine of the incarnation. And, as I

---

23. Sabina, interview by author, April 11, 2017.
24. Samira, interview by author, March 16, 2017.
25. Sigurdson, *Heavenly Bodies*.

A Theological Proposal for Embodied Agency

noted, he also discusses the idea of gaze, particularly the Christian "gaze of faith" that centers on God embodied in Jesus. Then, Sigurdson weaves these threads into a modern Christian theology of embodiment. He notes that embodiment is important to Christianity because of "the sacramental quality of the Christian faith."[26] Thus, materiality is the medium through which spirituality is mediated to humanity. For Christian widows in northern Nigeria, their contested bodies in the process of the mourning rituals can mediate Jesus' incarnational power that will lead to social change.

In his philosophical analysis of the body, Sigurdson also underscores the fact that embodiment rejects the Cartesian body experience.[27] Sigurdson notes that the body Rene Descartes had in mind was a corpse rather than a living body. In other words, only corpses can be analyzed objectively. What this means is that the theoretical understanding of the human body depends on a person's unique experience of her embodiment and not by abstracting thought from embodiment or detouring through scientific studies of the body. Thus, the widow's experience of her embodiment can be described by observing her unique interactions with the world around her.

Sigurdson discusses two important categories in the description of the phenomenal body: *spatiality* and *mobility*.[28] Spatiality states that one's body parts are not located side by side, but they are contained in each other.[29] In other words, the existence of one part of the body is the existence of the whole body. Sigurdson speaks of "situational" and "positional" spatiality. The former bespeaks the fact that one has space because one has a body. And the latter, which depends on situational spatiality, refers to the body's position within space. The second category that explains the phenomenal body is its mobility. According to Sigurdson, movement is the active seizing of space and time.[30] In other words, movement becomes the way that the body inhabits space. However, movement is impossible without spatiality. Concurrently, it is movement that makes spatiality possible.[31] Movement is a congruent part of the body.

Spatiality and movement were present in every conversation I had with the widows. I cannot remember how many times I heard widows saying

---

26. Sigurdson, *Heavenly Bodies*, 18.
27. Sigurdson, *Heavenly Bodies*, 301.
28. Merleau-Ponty, *Phenomenology of Perception*.
29. Sigurdson, *Heavenly Bodies*, 98.
30. Sigurdson, *Heavenly Bodies*, 110.
31. Merleau-Ponty, *Phenomenology of Perception*, 110–11.

they refused to leave their children before and after their husbands' deaths. In fact, widowhood influenced their movement. As widows, they occupied space that undermines their embodied agency. Evelyn suffered emotional and physical abuse by her husband. He refused to give her money for food; she had to do menial tasks to earn enough to feed their children. He drank and slept with prostitutes. She thought of leaving but remained for the children. After he died, she faced maltreatment at the hands of her in-laws, but, as she said, "I refused to leave my children."[32] But such a noble decision incapacitated Evelyn. Existing within a liminal reality meant she operated as a disembodied person because she became unconscious of her body.[33] Perhaps that is why her response to my question about agency was that only God can position her for social change.[34] Although I cited her response in chapter 3 as a positive posture towards embodied agency, I also observed that her demeanor suggested a sense of helplessness towards embodied agency. She believed in God but she was skeptical that God would use her to transform society. Her response highlights the fact that her disembodied body mediates the dualistic world in which she has been operating. In their theologizing, Christian widows recognize that such a "world" undermine their embodied agency.

A holistic vision recognizes that the widows' lived experiences change. EWS is providing some of that support to enable Evelyn to move into space towards reincorporation rather than continue to remain in liminality. The incarnation readily applies to the widows' realities because the incarnation suggests that Jesus occupied space within the creation. Jesus actively seized space and time to overturn human structures that undermined the flourishing of all creation. An embodied Christology also enables a Christian widow like Evelyn to overturn and transcend cultural norms that undermine her embodied agency.[35] Based on Sigurdson's assertion, Jesus' life exemplified resistance towards structures that undermine human flourishing. Evelyn is positioning herself to emulate such resistance by embodying the way mourning rituals will lead to social change.

My point is that widows' contested bodies can mediate God's transforming activities in the world. This is a position that is also congruent with feminist theologians. By critiquing the contestation of the bodies of Africa's

32. Evelyn, interview by author, April 13, 2017.
33. Sigurdson, *Heavenly Bodies*, 578.
34. Evelyn, interview by author, April 13, 2017.
35. McMillan, *Embodied Avatars*, 3.

A Theological Proposal for Embodied Agency

women, feminist theology demands that African women be given access to resources that position them to embody a brighter future for Africa. Feminist theologians ground widows' agency upon the incarnation of Jesus.

Feminist Theologies and Embodiment

Mercy Amba Oduyoye blazes the trail for scholarship on the issue of women's agency by examining the influence of culture and religion on women's experiences. In *African Women, Religion, and Health*, Isabel A. Phiri and Sarojini Nadar describe Oduyoye's key contributions to modern African theology, and then they apply her insights to issues such as health and poverty.[36] The essays in this volume reveal several perspectives on the ways that the African woman's body is being contested. In her article "From Mere Existence to Tenacious Endurance," Denise Ackerman unpacks the gendered nature of stigma and HIV both within the church and society.[37] Ackerman argues that this debate needs to take place in religious institutions, freeing it from cultural taboos and Christian teachings that have little understanding of embodiment.[38]

Of importance to this study, Ackerman notes that feminist theologies are interested in women's lives, which includes "their stories, their hopes, their beliefs, and their experiences of oppression and liberation."[39] Specifically, feminist theologies want to bring women's lives into the "drama of the Christian message and explore how Christian faith grounds and shapes women's experiences of hope, justice, and grace as well as instigating and enforcing women's experiences of oppression, sin, and evil."[40] Ackerman advocates for a feminist theology of praxis that points to intentional social activity. This feminist theology of praxis is predicated on human willingness to be God's representative in the world by alleviating oppression and creating communities of hope, perseverance, and new visions of what human flourishing entails.[41] This feminist theology of praxis is resolutely ethical and contextual; thus, it identifies women's sufferings and articulates potentialities of hope and transformation by locating them within a specific

---

36. Phiri and Nadar, *African Women, Religion, and Health*.
37. Ackerman, "From Mere Existence."
38. Ackerman, "From Mere Existence," 221–42.
39. Ackerman, "From Mere Existence," 225.
40. Ackerman, "From Mere Existence," 225.
41. Ackerman, "From Mere Existence," 226.

ethical framework.[42] In short, this historical and contextual theology recognizes the particularity and dissimilarity of rituals in its reflections on how Jesus' incarnation engenders women's embodied agency within Africa. This aligns with my position that widows can embody the ways mourning rituals will lead to social change by mediating the power of Jesus' incarnation.

In sum, Sigurdson and feminist theologians show a strong link between incarnation and embodiment as it pertains to African women. First, the interaction between incarnation and embodiment demonstrates the interaction between Christianity and social change. Therefore, Christian widows integrate their Christian faith and their experiences by embodying the ways mourning rituals will lead to social change. Second, it is not only my assessment that widows are integrating their Christian faith and embodied agency, but also the contention of Sigurdson and feminist theologians that embodiment is congruent with Christianity. Sigurdson and feminist theologians observe that Christians are mediators of God within society. Sigurdson's idea of moving into space aligns with Ackerman's contextualization, where Christians embody their agency within their specific contexts. As I demonstrate in this study, inculturation is a pertinent theme of embodiment. I show how inculturation is used by Christian widows to embody the ways mourning rituals will lead to social change. And third, Sigurdson and feminist theologians demonstrate the significance of understanding people's lived realities. In other words, the link between the incarnation and embodiment requires comprehending every aspect of widows' lives. What this underscore is the need for a holistic approach towards embodied agency.

What I want to do in this chapter is further unpack these three themes of embodiment in proposing how widows can embody the ways mourning rituals will lead to social change. I have demonstrated how faith and social change coincide; in fact, this study is the interaction between religion and the social context. Later in the chapter, I demonstrate how widows use inculturation to embody their mourning rituals towards social change. But I begin by showing how Christian widows use a holistic approach towards an embodied agency. I have shown how Pentecostalism engenders a holistic approach to guiding widows' agency. Here, I broker a conversation between African sociology and theology to buttress the need for Christian widows to use a holistic approach to development towards embodied agency that will lead to social change.

---

42. Ackerman, "From Mere Existence," 227.

A Theological Proposal for Embodied Agency

A Holistic Approach towards Embodied Agency

Cheryl Pridham tells this heart-wrenching story that illustrates the need for a holistic approach to development towards embodied agency that will lead to social change:

> We had a student whose parents wanted her to remarry. But she refused. Pretty soon, when men came to the school to look for wives from the widows, a man became interested in her. He went home to plan to marry her. But she insisted that she would not remarry. She would come over to our house, crying. And I would just say, "Tell your father you don't want this." But someone told me, "Don't tell her that. Her sister told them that if she would not marry the person they had chosen for her, in twenty-four hours, she was dead. She was killed by her own relatives because they poisoned her. So please stop telling her to refuse to remarry."[43]

What the story above demonstrates is that the pressures Christian widows face upon the deaths of their husbands are numerous and complex. These pressures lead to widows' disembodied existence. In other words, the pressures widows face place their bodies in a state of perpetual contestation. By that, I mean widows succumb to an unending cycle of maltreatment that undermines their capacity to effect social change. The story above also demonstrates that the pressures widows face have grave consequences. Thus, widows' inability to effect change is not only inhibited by their lack of social status but their physical deaths. GAWON and EWS emphasize the need to reclaim widows' bodies through a holistic Christian tradition that I suggest we also need to reclaim.

Because Africans place strong emphasis on religion and the body, reclaiming the body and Africa's thoroughly embodied, holistic Christian tradition and spiritual practices are vital. In his groundbreaking book *The Invention of Africa*, V. Y. Mudimbe addresses the diverse scholarly discourses by both Africans and non-Africans about the meaning of Africa and what it means to be an African.[44] Mudimbe gives a vivid and engaging description of the struggles of Africa's self-invention, arguing that the diverse discourses have influenced people's view of themselves and of Africa. He blames Western anthropologists and missionaries for introducing distortions about Africa and Africans.

---

43. Cheryl Pridham, interview by author, March 24, 2017.
44. Mudimbe, *Invention of Africa*.

Agents of Social Change

The distortions Mudimbe speaks about concerns the dualistic framework Western anthropologists and missionaries impose upon Africans. Mudimbe states that Africans give attention to the evolution implied in the Western and African dichotomies, which suggests a passage from one paradigm to another.[45] By this, Mudimbe is referring to the notion that elevates Western motifs as "developed" and African motifs as "underdeveloped." However, he cites that such evolution from "underdevelopment" to "development" is misleading.[46] Rather, Mudimbe states that between these two extremes is an intermediate space where the social and economic realities define the extent of marginality.[47] However, Mudimbe does not mention the "religious realities" since he blames Western anthropologists and missionaries for the dualistic approach, although he recognizes the importance of the religious realities of the intermediate state within which Africans exist.[48]

In citing several oppositions towards Western epistemology and its reductionist approach, Mudimbe suggests a resistance called "negritude," an intellectual and emotional sign of opposition to the ideology of white superiority.[49] Negritude affirms the value of African culture, heritage, and identity. According to Mudimbe, negritude champions "the warmth of existing in a natural, social, and *spiritual* harmony."[50] Therefore, despite his reservations about the ineffective role Christianity has played within Africa, he considers religion or spirituality pertinent to the future he anticipates for Africans. What Mudimbe recognizes is that the economic, social, and religious realities characterize the lived realities of Africans. However, religion is the most pertinent reality because it feeds the social and economic realities of widows. None of my respondents spoke about economic, social, and religious dimensions in isolation to the others, although widows view the social and economic dimensions through the prism of their Christian faith. Thus, religion is pertinent to a holistic approach of development towards

---

45. Mudimbe, *Africa's Dependence*.
46. Mudimbe, *Invention of Africa*, 4.
47. Mudimber, *Invention of Africa*, 4; See also Shaw, *Towards A Political Economy*.
48. As most Africans, Mudimbe differentiates the terms "religious" and "spiritual." However, I have no reason to do so because my respondents did not. Also, the literature provides no explanations of their differences. Mudimbe differentiates between the terms because he wishes to discard Western motifs, thereby establishing a pure African reality. Unlike Mudimbe, I am not willing to discard Western motifs. On the contrary, I suggest appropriating Western and African motifs.
49. Mudimbe, *Invention of Africa*, 93.
50. Mudimbe, *Invention of Africa*, 93.

embodied agency that will lead to social change in northern Nigeria. Through a holistic vision of embodied agency, Christian widows can appropriate Western and African motifs to embody mourning rituals that will lead to social change. What I am suggesting is that widows' bodies become "texts" that can mediate the power of Jesus' incarnation within society.

On Embodied Textuality

In her book *The Anthropology of Texts, Persons and Publics*, Karin Barber draws from Africa and other regions to explore textuality from a variety of angles.[51] She argues that oral and written texts evoke personhood, as she underscores the role of audience in creating meaning for texts. This demonstrates that textual creativity is a universal human capacity expressed in different forms. Perhaps the most impressive aspect of Barber's book is the depth, detail, and range of material on African verbal performance in social contexts, although there are also classic examples from elsewhere. For this study, Barber states that oral and written "texts also are things," which means they are social and historical facts whose forms, transformations, and dispersal can be studied empirically.[52] Barber's statement is the essence of embodiment: that people become texts that reveal the hopes and aspirations of society. This study stems from my empirical research of the lives of Christian widows in northern Nigeria to demonstrate that widowhood provides a unique angle for exploring textuality. What I found is that these widows are not just drawing upon Western and African motifs, they become "texts" that bear social and historical facts. Rita's imaginary lines on her body and Sabina's desire to know what is inside of her shows that widows consider their bodies as texts to mediate the power of Jesus' incarnation that will lead to social change.

Because I am examining embodiment through the lens of Jesus' incarnation, I discuss embodiment here from a theological standpoint. I weave the widows' stories to demonstrate how Christian widows can embody the ways mourning ritual will lead to social change by mediating the power of Jesus' incarnation. Incarnational theology has to do with God's active presence in human affairs. In the Bible, God is present in creation (Gen 1:2; Ps 104:30). The Hebrew Bible emphasizes the Wisdom of God that creates and sustains creation (Ps 93:2; Prov 8:22–23). However, there does not exist

---

51. Barber, *Anthropology of Texts*.
52. Barber, *Anthropology of Texts*, 200.

a "representation of incarnation in a Christological sense in the Hebrew Bible, as is self-evident, nor in the more general sense of God taking form in a concrete, embodied way in human history."[53] According to Sigurdson, the clearest and the most effective Christological representation of the incarnation is in the New Testament.

Sigurdson states that John's prologue offers a more developed Christology. In John's prologue, the Word of God is the activity of God and the personification of God. John refers to this as *logos* ("Word") that became human (John 1:1). Verse 14 signals the passage from the preexistence or impersonal personification of the Hebrew Bible to incarnation or an actual person. Therefore, John was not only concerned with Word or God's glory in human form. Rather, Sigurdson's focus was on Jesus as a "concrete, historical, and embodied person."[54] This liberating gospel is based on the premise that God "tabernacles" with us through Jesus Christ (John 1:14). The implication is that "Jesus' life on earth does not become an item of the historical past but constantly remains a present reality."[55]

The incarnation is not an event in Jesus' life; rather, the incarnation reflects the significance of a specific, distinctive narrative rather than one event within the narrative.[56] What this means for widows like Rita and Sabina is that they can mediate the power of Jesus' incarnation within their specific historical, cultural, and social circumstances.[57] This is what Beya means by the need for African women to inculturate the word of God.[58] By this, Beya refers to making the gospel relevant within diverse contexts. In other words, Jesus' life can be incarnated in Christian widows towards an embodied agency within the specific contexts of northern Nigeria. I demonstrate how inculturation is being used by widows towards embodied agency.

Inculturation towards Embodied Agency

Inculturation has to do with the widows' embodied agency that is culturally relevant to northern Nigeria. Most of the widows' responses about agency mentioned culturally relevant ways they can embody the ways mourning

53. Sigurdson, *Heavenly Bodies*, 57.
54. Sigurdson, *Heavenly Bodies*, 63.
55. Bultmann, *Theology of the New Testament*, 49.
56. Sigurdson, *Heavenly Bodies*, 66.
57. Sigurdson, *Heavenly Bodies*, 583.
58. Beya, "Human Sexuality," 178.

rituals will lead to social change. The literature also suggests that embodied agency requires ways to effect social change. There are four ways that Christian widows can embody the ways mourning rituals will lead to social change by mediating the power of Jesus' incarnation. In fact, the widows noted that words, singing/dancing, African art, and facial marks are the methods to embody the ways mourning rituals will lead to social change by mediating the power of Jesus' incarnation. I explain these ways from a Christian perspective.

Expressing Agency through Words

It is not surprising that most of the widows said they wanted to teach other widows and children in northern Nigeria. By teaching, the widows refer to the widows at EWS who use words to transform the lives of others. Words are pertinent to life in northern Nigeria. In northern Nigeria, *word* is understood as both dynamic and life-giving. Enyi Ben Udoh states that the *word* in Africa is "an act of affirming one's being in and commitment to a particular group of people. To participate in speech-event is to live. Therefore, not to speak up or speak out against social evil is to deny oneself this natural right."[59] Widows can embody transformation through speech because that is what it means to live. And widows cannot be representational voices, as I discussed in chapter 3, without speech. The word has the capacity to create and re-create any community because the word mirrors truthfulness, fairness, honesty, and communication.[60] By their speech, widows can relate the truth they have received. They will promote God's liberating Truth in Jesus.

It is important to note that the widows realized "teaching" others is part of their embodied agency towards social change. When she speaks at widows' events, Deborah Bonat said, "I show them how they must overcome the challenges of widowhood."[61] As she teaches the widows how to make soap, Bonat, a widow herself, uses words to challenge Christian widows to embody the ways mourning rituals will lead to social change by mediating the power of Jesus' incarnation. Barber's analysis, which allows texts to be understood as performances, breaks down the dichotomy between speech and bodies. In other words, Barber recognizes that textual meaning is produced within every culture through the interpretation of performing

---

59. Udoh, *Guest Christology*, 37.
60. Uzukwu, *Listening Church*, 127.
61. Deborah Bonat, interview by author, March 22, 2017.

either the oral or written texts.[62] Performance thus blurs the line between what is said or written and what is perceived by the agent. In performance, speech and bodies are one and the same. Thus, Christian widows like Bonat appropriate scripture by performing, speaking, and living out the power of Jesus' incarnation.

Expressing Agency through Singing and Dancing

When Asabe came home and found mourners, she was startled. But what she did when she was informed of her daughter's death amazed everyone. She said, "I didn't cry, I held my daughter's body and sang and danced to my heart's content. Then, I laid her down. People were shocked at my composed disposition. But I told them that this is the power of God."[63] She did not tell me what song she sang. It is possible that it was not a song she composed, but one that would have spoken directly to the situation in a powerful way. In *Performing Religion*, Gregory Barz uses *kwaya* ("choir") groups in Tanzania to demonstrate the combination of the cultural landscape.[64] Barz adopts an analytical approach for his study that is regularly utilized in the areas of ethnomusicology, religious studies, culture studies, and philosophy for understanding expanded social process-consciousness. For Barz, the *kwaya* is not just musical performance, but it is the "process of community formation, the process of communities performing themselves into being on a regular basis."[65]

Although Barz describes this phenomenon in East Africa, his arguments translate into the northern Nigerian context because music is integral to the life of northern Nigeria. Music not only serves to reveal people's lived realities, but it is also a tool towards social change. Thus, whether Asabe realized it or not, her musical performance did not only speak into her lived reality but contributed towards social change. Since it is probable that Asabe sang a familiar chorus, other people would have joined her in singing. For Christian widows in northern Nigeria, singing mediates the power of Jesus' incarnation. Singing initiates deeper contact with the divine. Such a divine encounter resulted in Asabe choosing to celebrate beauty rather than dwell in the pain of loss. Therefore, Asabe's decision to sing shocked

62. Barber, *Anthropology of Texts*, viii.
63. Asabe, interview by author, March 28, 2017.
64. Barz, *Performing Religion*.
65. Barz, *Performing Religion*, 14.

those who came to console her, thereby transforming them. By that, I mean she altered their perception of grief that day.

Because singing accompanies dancing in northern Nigeria, it is important to note that drums have a special place in African life. Dance is also integral to African life, and it is also a tool towards social change. Christian dance finds its validity in the Bible (2 Sam 6:5; 6:14–15; and Ps 150:3–4). In African churches, dances are performed during worship. In fact, some African churches play the drums to herald the coming of Christ during the sacrament of communion.[66] Joseph Osei-Bonsu suggests that only those gifted should dance since dance is not an entertainment, but a "medium for praising God and for fostering prayer."[67] Asabe also used her gift of dance to move from the space of grief into joy. By doing that, she demonstrated that Jesus' incarnation leads to desirable realities for society through the embodied agency of widows.

Expressing Agency through African Art

One of the courses the widows take at EWS is a sewing/knitting class. I observed some widows learning to sew clothes. Philomena, a young widow, was one of those widows. Philomena's response to my question about how learning to sew can enable her agency was, "I use my sewing skills to help people in my village."[68] She said she sewed Christmas clothes for children in her village. She has become notable for her contributions to the people of her community. Thus, being able to use her skills enables her to embody the ways mourning rituals lead to social change as she mediates the power of Jesus' incarnation.

Osei-Bonsu rejects modern depictions of Jesus that portray him as a man of multiple races.[69] Osei-Bonsu credits those depictions for their messages but points out that such an attempt aims to deny the historicity of Jesus. Rather, what is powerful about art is its symbolic function. To adequately express the gospel in their diverse contexts, Christian widows include the symbolism of art in church-worship. In their case, it might not be a painting on a canvas, but they nonetheless utilize their skills and gifts

---

66. Osei-Bonsu, *Inculturation of Christianity*, 114.
67. Osei-Bonsu, *Inculturation of Christianity*, 115.
68. Philomena, interview by author, April 22, 2017.
69. Osei-Bonsu, *Inculturation of Christianity*, 115.

to mediate the power of Jesus' incarnation within their contexts.[70] Christian widows such as Philomena utilize their creative capacities to reflect Jesus in tangible ways. These tangible manifestations could serve as reference points towards achieving social change.

Expressing Agency through Facial Markings

Binta's facial marks are hard to ignore. The two straight lines across her cheeks are tribal marks she received during her rite of passage into womanhood. Facial markings are commonplace among peoples of diverse ancestral categories of northern Nigeria.[71] Facial marks in forms of deep scarification are done for aesthetic, identification, and protection purposes. While facial marking is common among most of the various tribes in Nigeria, it is more pronounced among some. Different names are attached to different types of facial marks based on the number, breadth, and arrangement of the lines. These facial markings are used by northern Nigerian widows to transform society. What I mean is that facial markings are no longer considered a cultural marker but a spiritual marker that identifies them to the incarnation of Jesus. In other words, Christian widows can use facial marks to tell their story of transformation from culturally bounded to gracefully bonded to Jesus Christ. Binta, a young widow, explained that these tribal marks no longer defined who she was. "My identity is in Christ. All I can do is thank God."[72] I observed that several widows in the region have tribal facial marks, including the widows I interviewed. They do not consider those facial marks in purely cultural ways as they used to; rather, they consider those facial marks as a means towards embodied agency.

In sum, Barber notes that oral or written texts are interwoven to provide internal coherence. Barber also notes that the weaving of oral and written texts makes texts detachable from ongoing talk and action. What the weaving of oral and written texts involves is the process of "entextualization." Entextualization combines fixity and fluidity, thereby allowing the processes of imitation and creativity to occur simultaneously. Entextualization engenders inculturation because appropriation of oral and written texts requires both imitation and creativity. In other words, Christian widows can imitate and (re)create the power of the incarnation within

70. Osei-Bonsu, *Inculturation of Christianity*, 116.
71. Ibeabuchi, "Body Painting Art."
72. Binta, interview by author, April 12, 2017.

A Theological Proposal for Embodied Agency

northern Nigeria as they embody the ways mourning rituals will lead to social change.

Mourning Ritual, the Incarnation, and Embodied Agency

While examining Victor Turner's *The Ritual Process* in chapter 2, I noted that Turner demonstrates that rituals have become central arenas towards social change. Rosemary N. Edet states that rituals are ways people "control, construct, order, fashion or create ways to be fully humans."[73] For this reason, she notes that rituals are necessary because they engender *shalom*.[74] By that, Edet concurs with Victor Turner's assertion that rituals become means towards social change. Therefore, the mourning rituals can lead to social change. This is the basis of my theoretical framework in this study.

In chapter 2, I also highlighted Turner's three phases in the rite of passage: separation, margin, and aggregation. Three characteristics of the mourning rituals correspond to Turner's three phases: the mourning dress, the mourning period, and the mourning celebration. I draw upon the three phases of Turner's rite of passage to propose a theology for the embodied agency of Christian widows in northern Nigeria. A theology of embodied agency is necessary because Christian religious principles engender widows' agency. My proposal is that Christian widows can embody the ways mourning rituals will lead to social change by mediating the power of Jesus' incarnation.

Embodying the Mourning Dress towards Social Change

Turner states that "separation" involves symbolic behavior that heralds a person's detachment from the group/individual, from a state in social structure and/or from a set of cultural conditions. What this means for the widow is that her mourning dress identifies her as one separated from a state she once was. This identity involves separating her from freely interacting with people she needs to help her thrive. The widow is forced to dwell in the breach that the death of her husband brings to her. Further, the dress is not meant only to separate her from society, but to expose her body to society's gaze. Therefore, the mourning dress represents a separation

---

73. Edet, "Christianity," 26.
74. Edet, "Christianity," 26.

that undermines widows' agency by shaming widows. The dress separates widows from the life they once lived and the life they desire for themselves, their children, and for society.

When Tamara's husband died, he left her with nothing to care for six young children. During our interview, she narrated the hopelessness she still feels as she described the deplorable nature of her situation. In our interaction, I noticed the impact separation had on her. By inviting me into her home, she "undressed" herself to me by telling me her problems and allowing me to see her in her grief-stricken state. Only her family and friends are supposed to see her in such a state, not a stranger like me.[75] In fact, as someone she was meeting for the first time, tradition demands for her to entertain me. But the dress of mourning prevents her from doing so, since she is required to only sit in mourning. She is separated from society by the laws governing widowhood and the shame that accompanies widowhood. Understanding this, she repeated a phrase multiple times: *Allah zai rufe mani asiri* ("God will cover my secrets").[76] In fact, Tamara said, "God is helping us." Widows like Tamara attribute their ability to cope with the challenges of widowhood to "God's grace." Therefore, EWS and GAWON make the "spiritual aspect" of developing these Christian widows a priority. By making the spiritual aspect a priority, what these organizations desire is for widow's mourning dress to become a symbol that inspires society to anticipate the hope for justice in northern Nigeria.

There was a constant refrain among the widows that is applicable here. Seventy-five percent of the widows referred to the need for the widow to *kame kanta* ("hold her body"). The expression refers to a person's temperament; it means "self-control" or "disciplined." Felicia states that in her separation from society, she refused to participate in dubious activities as some widows did; rather, she said, "I took my body, and held it."[77] The recurrent advice that veteran widows offer to young widows is to "hold their bodies." The veteran widows suggest that by holding their bodies young widows reflect what it means to depend on God. The correlation between holding one's body and trusting the Lord was apparent in most of the responses of both the veteran and young widows. Zhowi states, "If widows hold their bodies and trust in the Lord . . . God will provide for them."[78] In a sense,

---

75. I could see her because I was acquainted with a respectable member of the family.
76. Tamara, interview by author, March 26, 2017.
77. Felicia, interview by author, March 16, 2017.
78. Zhowi, interview by author, March 16, 2017.

A Theological Proposal for Embodied Agency

separation is an opportunity for widows to embody God's ability to provide what society needs to be transformed. Thus, even within the separation of their widowhood as symbolized by the mourning dresses, widows can effect social change by mediating the power of Jesus' incarnation.

Fundamentally, *kame kanta* also suggests that widows should accept their plights. Jummai said, "The struggles most widows face is their inability to accept what has happened to them."[79] By accepting the fact that their husbands are dead, Christian widows accept the dress of widowhood as pertinent towards social change. In fact, Jummai emphasized that accepting their predicaments is vital towards embracing widows' calling as agents of transformation within society. Therefore, accepting what has happened to them means seeing the "dress of separation" through the lens of Jesus' incarnation, which anticipates healing and transformation for the widow and for society. Felicia accepted the dress of widowhood towards embodied agency that will lead to social change. She does not only work to provide for her children but for the children of other widows. Felicia embodies the hope for the future while abiding in suffering.

Before I venture further, let me show the implication of embodying the mourning dress towards social change. By becoming human, Jesus wore the dress of broken humanity to identify with humanity in their separation with God while initiating reconciliation with God. In other words, Jesus' humanity leads to a victorious future for broken humanity. The widow's hope for a victorious future is symbolized in the mourning dress. For while the black or white dresses widows are required to wear symbolize mourning, black also symbolizes age and maturity in northern Nigeria. The color white also symbolizes peace and victory. This symbolism highlights the fact that Jesus' incarnation came at the "right time," bespeaking maturity; and the incarnation is God's way of giving us victory.

Embodying the Mourning Period towards Social Change

Turner's focus on the liminal phase of the rite of passage is noteworthy. As I stated in chapter 2, Turner considers the liminal phase the most neglected in the classifications of states within cultural space. But the liminal phase cannot be ignored within the reality of widowhood in northern Nigeria since it occurs in all characteristics of mourning rituals. I also noted in chapter 2 that mourning periods that last between three and twelve months

---

79. Jummai, interview by author, March 24, 2017.

because mourning periods happen in stages. What the liminal phase highlights are the pains associated with the widows' rite of passage, which demands for widows to endure the suffering in hope.

Sixty percent of the widows referred to *natsuwa* ("keeping steady"). Technically, *natsuwa* and *kame kanta* mean the same thing. In fact, one widow referred to the need for both *kame kanta* and *natsuwa* during our conversation. However, while *kame kanta* primarily refers to "self-control," *natsuwa* primarily means "concentration." I observed that while *kame kanta* has to do with maintaining an attitude of hope in suffering, *natsuwa* has to do with maintaining an attitude of suffering in hope. In other words, the former focuses on the future, while the latter focuses on the present.[80] The widows are encouraged to concentrate on the process of widowhood to help people see their challenges as springboards towards embodied agency that will lead to social change. Sandra spoke about how she is concentrating on the process towards embodied agency: "Although the tendency is to ask God to take away my sufferings, I use my situation to encourage other people."[81] Sandra spoke as a widow who not only lost her husband but lost all her property to her in-laws. She tried to regain the property but was powerless against her well-connected in-laws. Lacking formal education and marketable skills, Sandra depends on organizations like GAWON for her upkeep and the upkeep of her children. She is focused on the process towards embodied agency with an amazing view of hope amid her challenges.

What I discovered is that the widows' challenges involve the persistence of grief. Society assumes the widow's grief is exhausted after the traditionally allotted time; however, her grief continues for several years after the mourning period. Anita's story proves this point. Years after her husband's death, Anita recounted the first time she came to EWS: "I cried a lot, I was depressed. I cried every day. By God's grace, I became strong . . . but I cried a lot."[82] Widows like Anita never fully come to terms with the

---

80. I should also note that the closeness of the words *natsuwa* and *kame kanta* highlight the interrelationship between the mourning dress and the mourning period. But I also use them separately here because, while widows like Sandra have completed the mourning period required by tradition, they live in perpetual mourning. Turner attributes this societal assumption to the fact that liminality has an ambiguous characteristic. He states that liminality leads to invisibility, which refers to a widow lacking accessibility to society's resources; darkness, which refers to the widow's gloomy reality; and death, which refers to her being forgotten by society.

81. Sandra, interview by author, March 16, 2017.

82. Anita, interview by author, March 16, 2017.

"ugliness" of their misfortunes because society manipulates the mourning period. Because the ugliness of widowhood is unavoidable, several widows would admit to still be crying. If they are unable to come to terms with their widowhood, they would not be able to concentrate on the process of their embodied agency.

However, by highlighting "God's grace," Anita recognizes the power of Jesus' incarnation in the process of her embodied agency. Widows like Anita demonstrate that their never-ending grief is also life-changing for them, and, consequently, for society. In describing Jesus, the prophet Isaiah states, "He had no beauty or majesty to attract us to him, nothing in his appearance that we should desire him" (53:2b). Isaiah used active verbs to describe the Messiah's pain: "despised," "rejected," "pierced," "crushed," "oppressed," and "afflicted." These verbs are evident of the widows' reference to *natsuwa*. The widows experience a pain like that of Jesus. I am not equating their pain to that of Jesus but underscoring that Jesus' suffering gives meaning to theirs. In other words, they can embody the grief of the mourning period that has the potential to lead to social change.

When I accompanied some widows to the market, I observed the way Jesus' suffering gives meaning to widows' suffering in northern Nigeria. I noticed that everyone stared at them. While most people looked at them with disdain, I also noticed that others looked admiringly at them, perhaps inspired by the widows' endurance despite their sufferings. The former is culturally accepted, but the latter is unacceptable, since widowhood suggests a loss of personhood. Yet, such a positive response towards widows underscores the potential that widows have in transforming northern Nigeria. As a suffering servant, Jesus also had people who despised him; however, others were drawn to the beauty they experienced in his sufferings. And when they accepted the value of Jesus' suffering for themselves, they were transformed.

By accepting the value of Jesus' suffering, widows who maintain an attitude of suffering in hope choose joy as they embody hope for society. For, as they embrace *natsuwa*, Christian widows are overcoming the invisibility, darkness, and death of the liminal phase while hoping for the consummation of their sufferings. They can embody the sufferings and pains of the mourning rituals that will lead to social change by mediating the power of Jesus' incarnation. Simply, the widows can become symbols of resistance towards the injustices that permeates society, as they anticipate a brighter future for society.

Agents of Social Change

Embodying the Mourning Celebration towards Social Change

The reason mourning periods happen in stages is because the mourning rituals are considered "celebrations," although my description demonstrates that widowhood is anything but a celebration for the widows. However, at the culmination of the mourning ritual, a ceremony is held. It is fair to argue if the ceremony at the end of the mourning ritual is also a celebration, since it requires the widow to use her meager resources to entertain people that come to mourn with her. Turner refers to this third phase of the rite of passage as "reaggregation" or "reincorporation."[83] This is when the widow is said to be in a relatively stable state, which accords her the rights and obligations of a clearly defined and "structural" type. In other words, the widow is expected to trade her mourning dress for her celebratory dress. Singing and dancing constitutes her reincorporation within society. Most of the women who were at Asabe's home to mourn her daughter were also present during the ceremony of her completing the mourning rituals. They welcomed Asabe into relationship with them towards embodied agency. Therefore, the celebration of the completion of the mourning rituals becomes a significant moment for widows' embodied agency that can lead to social change by mediating the power of Jesus' incarnation.

Asabe and the women belong to the "women fellowship choirs" (*zumuntan mata*) that are found across churches in northern Nigeria. These *zumuntan mata* choirs meet weekly to define their spirituality musically. Their music includes singing, praying, receiving, and passing along faith traditions. The choir also accords them the ability to negotiate change. As Osei-Bonsu noted about the need for Africans to compose songs that speak into their lived realities,[84] widows negotiate change by composing songs that speak to the issues that permeate society. At EWS, for instance, chapel begins with a chorus that calls on God to help the widow overcome temptations: *Allah ka tuna da ni chikin mulkinka* ("God remember me in your kingdom"). This song, composed by the widows, speaks to the marginalization that widowhood brings to them. This prayerful song is based on the temptations widows face to survive widowhood. They pray that God will not forget them but will position them to effect social change within northern Nigeria.

---

83. Turner, *Ritual Process*, 94–95.
84. Osei-Bonsu, *Inculturation of Christianity*, 114.

A Theological Proposal for Embodied Agency

The *zumuntan mata* choirs become pertinent towards widows' embodied agency because music is a major way that Christian widows express agency in northern Nigeria.[85] Barz proposes that we address the rigid boundaries around the study of arts in African expressive religious traditions. Barz notes that boundaries break down within the everyday performance of East African *kwayas*, since repositories, customs, antiquities, and traditions interact within a performance to enhance social identity. In other words, *kwayas* promote life. In northern Nigeria, music is salient to life. Bauta Motty notes that African cultures have celebrations because life is considered a journey; thus, to prevent singing and dancing is equivalent to death.[86] Christian widows in northern Nigeria express music through instruments and *wakoki* ("songs"). Music is the way that values and meanings are shared, a tool towards social change in northern Nigeria. We do not hear a lot about singing in the Gospels. However, Jesus would have heard or participated in singing several times. If he attended weddings (John 2), then he would have encountered singing. Moreover, the Gospels tell us that Jesus and his disciples sang hymns (Matt 26:30; Mark 14:26).

In northern Nigeria, dance takes different forms and expresses different types of meanings. Dance can be for psychological, religious, educational, biological, and social reasons.[87] In other words, dance can aid one to cope with aggression; communicate with spiritual forces; reinforce relationships; pass on values, traditions, and beliefs; and give one equilibrium.[88] Dancing must have accompanied the music in which Jesus participated. It should not be hard to imagine Jesus dancing, as dancing was part of the Jewish culture. He would have emulated his ancestor, David, whose dance is recorded in the Bible (Exod 15:20–21; 2 Sam 6:14; Ps 30:11; 149:3). Christian widows can use dance to move into both literal and metaphoric spaces that position them to effect social change in northern Nigeria.

Singing and dancing open public spaces for (re)negotiating injustices and transforming lives within everyday lived realities. Because the widow's body is never in neutral, movement transcends the challenges she faces.

---

85. It is important to note that the reason music is the major way widows express agency is because music involves words, arts, and facial markings. Because music involves the other ways widows express agency, it enables widows to be adaptable and flexible in the ways they embody the mourning rituals that leads to social change by reflecting the power of Jesus' incarnation.

86. Motty, *Indigenous Christian Disciple-Making*, 237.

87. Motty, *Indigenous Christian Disciple-Making*, 238.

88. Motty, *Indigenous Christian Disciple-Making*, 238.

This is exemplified by Asabe, who moved into the space of joy rather than grief by choosing to "live doxologically." In my conversations with the widows, I observed a deep sense of gratitude in the expression *na gode wa Allah* ("I thank God"). This is what I mean by "living doxologically." Widows like Asabe are grateful to God because they are alive to continue embodying God's grace within society. Moreover, choosing to live with gratitude anticipates the victory I described in chapter 4. Gloria says it best: "If I am not grateful to God for my life as a widow, then I do not know anything."[89] What she means is that God's grace reassures her that a bright future is possible. Therefore, she chooses to embody the ways mourning rituals can lead to social change in northern Nigeria by mediating the power of Jesus' incarnation. Two concepts highlight how the widow chooses to live doxologically in northern Nigeria: *forgiveness* and *peacemaking*.

Embodying Forgiveness

In his book *No Future without Forgiveness*, Desmond Tutu argues that genuine reconciliation recognizes past injustices to create a bright future.[90] However, he notes that it is not easy for a nation or individuals to "look the beast in the eye." He avoids cliché about forgiveness by providing a bold spirituality that acknowledges the atrocities people can inflict upon others while holding to a sense of idealism about reconciliation.

Martha narrated how her husband maltreated her. He ignored her and the children, making them sleep in a room with a leaky roof. When it rained, she and the children slept on their feet. There were times when her husband refused to give her money for food, forcing her to go to bed hungry. Before his death, he asked her for forgiveness for maltreating her. She paused, reliving the maltreatment she endured. But, as other widows, she said, "I erased everything he did to me from my heart."[91] That is a poignant response to years of maltreatment. In his reflection of Tutu's thoughts, John Inazu states that personal forgiveness is a necessary condition for political forgiveness, cautioning that group forgiveness should not coerce personal or political forgiveness.[92] Inazu also adds that personal forgiveness requires

---

89. Gloria, interview by author, April 24, 2017.
90. Tutu, *No Future without Forgiveness*.
91. Martha, interview by author, March 24, 2017.
92. Inazu, "No Future without (Personal) Forgiveness," 309–26.

A Theological Proposal for Embodied Agency

a shared narrative framework to lead to political forgiveness.[93] What this suggests is that society needs the participation of widows in the process of both personal and political forgiveness to attain a bright future. Widows like Martha can contribute to attaining this bright future by embodying the ways mourning rituals will lead to social change as they mediate the power of Jesus' incarnation.

Emmanuel Katongole states that forgiveness gives the person wronged a choice to be free from those past wrongs by creating her own path.[94] He also asserts that the incarnation names a different vision and story of power through Jesus; this vision and story provide a "distinctive possibility and *telos* of what a new future in Africa might look like."[95] The participation of widows in the process of forgiveness is necessary for a different vision and story for northern Nigeria. In a region that continues to be marred by ethno-religious violence, Christian widows can be catalysts towards sustainable peace in the region. And, as I mentioned in chapter 3, African women are seen as mediators of Africa's peace.

Embodying Peace

In "Women and Peacemaking: The Challenge of a Non-Violent Life," Susan Rokoczy emphasizes the peacemaking endeavors by both individual women and women-groups.[96] She maintains that even though Christianity has frequently been used to defend war, its preeminent tenet is one of peace. Rokoczy's point is that if Jesus was a peacemaker, African women are to embody peace. Rokoczy shares the stories of a couple of women engage in peacemaking efforts. While highlighting the work of South African women in the peacemaking process, she also notes the efforts of several African women towards peace during conflicts.

I found that widows desire to embody peace within society. They are mindful of the persistence of violence within their communities and desire to embody peace. According to Joy, it takes not only knowing the word of God but "my desire is that widows would live out the word of God as I have come to learn it."[97] It is safe to assert that what she learns include how

---

93. Inazu, "No Future without (Personal) Forgiveness," 309–26.
94. Veritas Forum, "Learning to Live with our Enemies."
95. Katongole, *Sacrifice of Africa*, 131.
96. Rokoczy, "Women and Peacemaking," 187–207.
97. Joy, interview by author, March 22, 2017.

pertinent it is to harmonize her life to Jesus, the prince of peace. Widows believe their faith challenges them to bring harmony to society. Rakoczy states that pacifism is an "effective means to change minds and hearts, to oppose policies that violate gospel principles, and to actively change situations that make war and violence possible."[98] According to Katongole, Christian widows need to embody Jesus' peace by refusing to become other actors in the triangle of violence.[99] In other words, Christian widows need to be part of the resistance to unjust societal structures through non-violent means. The widows demonstrated a readiness to become agents of social change in northern Nigeria through peacemaking.

In sum, Christian widows can embody the ways mourning rituals will lead to social change by mediating the power of Jesus' incarnation. Such an approach follows Jesus' example of enduring suffering in anticipation of joy. Rather than a symbol of oppression, Jesus transformed the cross to a symbol of freedom. Note that by undergoing the ritual of death on a cross, Jesus embodied resistance towards oppression while embodying embrace towards freedom. By doing so, Jesus reset humanity on a course towards a brighter future. As I said earlier, I am not equating the challenges of Christian widows to that of Jesus. What I am highlighting here is the fact that these widows consider Jesus an exemplar. Therefore, I suggest that Christian widows should view their challenges through the lens of Jesus' suffering. By doing so, the widows can embody the ways mourning rituals will lead to social change by mediating the power of Jesus' incarnation. Particularly, they will embody forgiveness and peace in a region plagued by ethno-religious crises.

To conclude, I will illustrate an instance where widows embodied how mourning rituals can lead to social change by mediating the power of Jesus' incarnation. I had the chance to attend a thanksgiving service to observe Christian widows participate in worship. The widows were all dressed up with yellow blouses and yellow/red wrappers and scarves; some widows wore jewelry, while others did not. Their colorful attire enlivened the room, overshadowing the deformed wooden benches and cracked floors. The sunlight that peered through the church's three doors and six windows accentuated the glare of their outfits. The widows were placed in the middle aisle seats, making them the center of focus and admiration. They formed the *zumunta mata* at the event. Accompanied by musical instruments and

98. Rakoczy, "Women and Peacemaking," 196–97.
99. Katongole, *Sacrifice of Africa*, 131.

A Theological Proposal for Embodied Agency

dance, they sang two songs. The introductory song was more subdued: *Kada ka barni in ja da baya* ("Please do not let me backslide"). The song pleads for God to help widows overcome the challenges of life that might lead them to vices. In fact, most widows tend to pray for grace through widowhood. Their prayer is based on the belief that widowhood is a calling to mediate the power of Jesus' incarnation.

But it was their second song that was more poignant because it encapsulates their embodied agency that can lead to social change in northern Nigeria. The refrain was:

> *Kai, wanda irin mutum kai, wanda irin mutum, kai*
> (You, what kind of person, what kind of person, you?)
> *Kai ba zafi ba, kai ba sanyi ba*
> (You are not hot, you are not cold)
> *Zan zubasda kai daga bakina*
> (I will spit you out of my mouth)
> *Kana da ido, baka gani?*
> (Do you have eyes, and not see?)
> *Kana da kunne, baka ji?*
> (Do you have ears, and not hear?)
> *Baka rayuwa kaman Yesu da kanache kana bi*
> (You are not living like the Jesus you profess to believe in)

The song is inspired by Jesus' words to the Laodicean church in Revelation 3:16. The Lord told the Laodicean church that the church was feigning they are rich, when the reality is that the Laodicean church was "wretched, pitiable, poor, blind and naked." Thus, Jesus called the church to buy gold from him to be rich, to put on white robes to cover their shame, and anoint their eyes with salve to see. Because widows believe their widowhood is a calling, the song suggests that widowhood has given these widows a vision of what true riches are. It is not in the abundance of material possession, but it is in submission to the Lord. Therefore, when widows speak about "God's help" or "God's grace," they anticipate that they can embody God's providential grace within society to engender social change.

Laodicea is the only church that Jesus exhorts to both hear and see. And the widows called society to do likewise. The widows challenged Christians towards complete devotion to God's principles. In the church that day, the widows were the lowest in the social hierarchy. However, their movements into space and their songs reverberated across the room, disarming us of our positions and power. Their movements and songs paralyzed every societal structure that marginalizes them. Everyone, including the elites (i.e., church leaders, elders, and dignitaries) at the event were captivated by how the widows embodied the way mourning ritual can lead to social change as they mediated the power of Jesus' incarnation. The widows used their bodies to beckon society towards a transformative existence. Their song and dance brought the past into the present in anticipation of unrelenting hope for northern Nigeria.

Conclusion

Christian widows in northern Nigeria embody the ways mourning ritual will lead to social change by mediating the power of Jesus' incarnation. The strong link between embodiment and the incarnation demonstrates that Christianity engenders social change. In other words, Christian widows recognize that their faith is futile if it does not lead to social change. To achieve social change, Christian widows use a holistic approach to development towards embodied agency. What that means is that they draw upon diverse motifs within society to effect social change. Moreover, Christian widows use biblical and culturally relevant ways to embody the ways mourning rituals will lead to social change by mediating the power of Jesus' incarnation. In other words, they are embodying the power of the incarnation in ways that are relevant to their specific contexts. A vision of societal change necessitates enlightenment by the incarnation of Jesus Christ; thus, society turns into a sphere for collective theologizing, with embodiment being a major area of conversation.

Conclusions

THIS STUDY SUGGESTS THAT religion engenders the agency of Christian widows towards social change in northern Nigeria. Investigating how Christian widows become agents of social change requires a discourse between theology and the social sciences. Specifically, it requires understanding the prominent ways that religion and widowhood practices impact conversations on the themes of agency, institutions, and embodiment. In each theme, an interaction between the social sciences and theology emerged that aimed to empower Christian widows for agency toward social change in northern Nigeria. The implication of this process is that widowhood provides an avenue for comprehending a theology of embodiment.

Since widowhood in northern Nigeria fundamentally has to do with a lack of power regarding the widows' orientation towards religious tenets, this study considered the theme of religion and its central role in the widows' lives. A life that is ordered by religious tenets required discussion of some preeminent characteristics of widowhood, which include sentiments, experiences, and rituals. I pointed out that northern Nigeria's history consists of religious sentiments that shape the lives of Christian widows. Northern Nigerian society projects religious sentiments upon everything, including widowhood. Therefore, religion shapes the experiences of Christian widows in northern Nigeria; these experiences are embraced because widowhood practices are considered "rites of passage" for widows. Unfortunately, such practices tend to disempower widows, leaving them to exist within the liminal phase of their rites of passage throughout their lives.

Based on this perspective, I described the dynamics of religion to widowhood in northern Nigeria. The study disclosed a set of themes (religion, agency, institution, and embodiment) that augment the widowhood experiences. These themes inform religious tenets, but religion also shapes and reshapes these themes through the concept of gaze. In fact, my goal for proposing an embodied theology revolves around the issue of gaze. In describing how religion undergirds widowhood practices, this study demonstrates that society does not "see" the widow. To inspire the widows' agency recognizes their potential to effect social change. Institutions that effectively guide widows' agency are those who make the widow feel she is "seen" by acknowledging that the Holy Spirit enables widows to attain spiritual insight and assume leadership roles within society. In short, Christian widows can embody the power of Jesus' incarnation towards social change.

What I mean is that society must recognize that these widows have the capacity to draw from their appropriations of the Spirit to contribute towards transforming society. Thus, because sight has a reciprocal dimension,[1] African societies need to exchange gazes with the widow. Both feminist theologians and social scientists are not advocating that society should stop gazing at widows. What they are suggesting is that such a gaze should be about finding ways to empower widows to gaze back at society in a constructive way. Empowering widows must ensure that they are able to gaze at society to contribute towards transforming it. In other words, society's gaze must be to empower widows and engender their agency in society.

I noted in chapter 3 that the experiences of African women revolve around relationships. The ability to gaze enhances an active relationship between the widow and the world around her.[2] It is no wonder that several authors suggest that alienation is the gravest challenge that widows in northern Nigeria face.[3] Being in relationship with and within society is empowering to widows. In fact, widows endure widowhood practices because they anticipate their integration into society. In short, they choose to abide in their suffering because they anticipate a future where they are restored

---

1. Sigurdson, *Heavenly Bodies*, 152.
2. Sigurdson, *Heavenly Bodies*, 152.
3. Bonat, "Challenges of Widowhood," 2; Adamu, *Nasarar Gwamruwa Kirista*; Taidi, *The Widow*.

Conclusions

back into relationship with and within society. Because religion plays a key role in the lived realities of widows, gaze must be viewed theologically.

Sigurdson provides a theological viewpoint of gaze. He explores New Testament perspective on gaze in relation to the understanding of Jesus, and the different depictions of Jesus, particularly within the theology of the icon and its implications.[4] He then draws the diverse aspects of gaze into a theological formulation of the specific gaze of Christianity in connection to the issue of Jesus' incarnation. What Jesus taught about sight and the implications for comprehending sight in multiple New Testament texts is Sigurdson's focus; it is equally my goal in drawing the conclusion of this study.

Sigurdson highlights several New Testament texts where we see the theme of sight coming to the forefront.[5] He explains gaze based on Jesus' emotion. In other words, he expresses that Jesus' gaze included sorrow, wrath, and love. Sigurdson also explains that Jesus healed blind people and encountered people who were spiritually blind. Sigurdson does not bring up this story, but, for the sake of this study, I would like to consider the widow of Nain in Luke 7:11–17 to draw out the implications of the concept of gaze as it pertains to empowering Christian widows for social change in northern Nigeria. Jesus' encounter with the widow of Nain suggests the presence of a generous gaze on Jesus' part, where he "sees" people considered marginal in society. By seeing them, Jesus also gives them the gift of his generous gaze.

While entering Nain, Jesus meets a funeral procession. Luke notes that the dead man is his mother's only son, and she is also a widow. In a highly patrilineal context, where women are identified in connection to men, this is a poignant reality. She is not only lonely, but she is without a protector and provider. Her chances for employment are very limited.[6] Thus, she is most likely going to enter some type of levirate arrangement as demanded by the law of Moses.[7] But levirate marriage consists of much uncertainty. For instance, you need a relative who wants you and who also has the means to care for you.

---

4. Sigurdson, *Heavenly Bodies*, 182.

5. These texts include Matthew 9:36, 27–31; Mark 3:5; John 11; Matthew 5–7; and Luke 2.

6. Morris, "Luke," 152.

7. Kalmin, "Levirate Law," 4:296.

Agents of Social Change

Luke does not mention professional mourners, but they would have been there since the law requires it (Ketub. 4:4). The large crowd suggests she has earned the sympathy of the people who are aware of her plight. Jesus is also moved with compassion for her and consoles her. But his consolation stems from his power to restore what she has lost. Joel B. Green notes that Jesus' miraculous power is Luke's focus.[8] Such power can turn sorrow to joy, shatter the boundaries of ritual purity,[9] and revive people.[10] The crowds glorified God by referring to Jesus as a "great prophet." This is evident by the fact that Luke uses the word "Lord" to refer to Jesus for the first time in this story.[11] And this is significant because what Luke points out is that true greatness involves a "seeing" that leads to restoration.

Most of the literature on the raising of the widow's son focuses on some of the points I discussed, but they overlook Jesus' generous gaze towards the widow. In other words, they failed to emphasize the fact that Jesus' compassion and restoration for the widow is preceded by the fact that Jesus "saw her." Sigurdson acknowledges that Jesus' compassion towards people bespeaks a seeing of their horrible realities.[12] Jesus is not just aware of her plight but is aware that widows belong to the lowest group in the society. Thus, the widow represents the "poor" to whom Jesus brings good news.[13] The levir is supposed to provide the care she needs to avoid the exploitation of others within society. However, exploitation happens. By seeing her, Jesus denounces those exploiting widows (Mark 12:40; Luke 20:47).

Sigurdson draws two overarching conclusions on gaze that are applicable to Christian widows in northern Nigeria. First, Sigurdson concludes that the New Testament provides diverse approaches to considering the issue of sight.[14] In short, sight is prominent in the New Testament. For this study, Jesus' encounter with the widow at Nain represents one such sighting. Jesus' approach in this story presents a peculiar sighting towards a woman who has lost every will to live. Her plight represents the plights of Christian widows in northern Nigeria today. And Christian widows in northern Nigeria

---

8. Green, "Gospel of Luke," 291.

9. Only the relatives of the dead can have any contact with the corpse or the bier ("coffin"). Therefore, Jesus makes himself ceremonially unclean.

10. Green, "Gospel of Luke," 292.

11. Morris, "Luke," 154.

12. Sigurdson, *Heavenly Bodies*, 185.

13. Green, "Gospel of Luke," 289–90.

14. Sigurdson, *Heavenly Bodies*, 205.

Conclusions

have also encounter Jesus as the widow of Nain did. What Christian widows in northern Nigeria need from society is the type of gaze Jesus accorded the widow at Nain, the generous gaze to which Sigurdson points.

Second, there is deep emotion attached to Jesus' gaze. In fact, compassion is foundational to Jesus' actions.[15] Sigurdson distinguishes between a "covetous gaze" and a "generous gaze." The former is the type of gaze Jesus shuns because such a gaze is instrumental in controlling people.[16] Jesus' compassionate spirit endorses a generous gaze. Such a gaze is also a gift given to those who enjoy communion with God such as Christian widows. The generous gaze helped the widow of Nain to see the coming kingdom of God connected with Jesus. Thus, Jesus helps Christian widows to see God's kingdom and gives them the gift of gaze. Because Jesus embodies God's reign, Christian widows see exactly who God is. This is a gift because by seeing God they are generated into God's likeness (2 Cor 3:18). And what this likeness demands is the widows' embodied agency.

Thus, beholding God's kingdom through Jesus engenders the widows' agency. The implications of this statement are twofold. First, Jesus gives the widow back her son (v. 15). However, Jesus does not only restore the life of the widow's son, but Jesus also restores the widow back to her society.[17] In short, the seeing of the widow is restorative. To empower Christian widows, society needs to look at them in a restorative manner. In other words, society must see the widow not as a person to be exploited, but as one to be empowered towards embodied agency.[18] Making her body an object of public morality is not empowering; it is disempowering because it perpetuates the objectification of her body. And objectifying her allows for practices that harm and marginalize her. What African societies need is to reorient their thinking towards widows. They must see widows as "assets," not "burdens," to society. For Christians, a "kingdom of vision" is one that regards the value of every member of society who, when given a chance, has the capacity to effect societal change. But we must "see" people through the lenses of the kingdom of God to engender their agency in northern Nigeria.

15. Luz, *Matthew 8–20*, 313–14.
16. Sigurdson, *Heavenly Bodies*, 208.
17. Green, "Gospel of Luke," 290.
18. On the other hand, we must avoid sacralizing the widows. As I noted, I encountered widows who supported the ill-treatment of other widows. I was also informed of widows who abandoned their children to marry another man. For this study, I focus on the positive aspects of the widow's experiences.

Second, Jesus gives the widow the gift of gaze. This concurs with Sigurdson about the reciprocity in gaze, whereby we allow what we see to see us. In seeing God's kingdom, the widow was gifted with gaze. For Luke, this is an important Christological theme: that Jesus also sees the people with whom society refuses to share their gift of gaze. Luke makes the widow central to the narrative to underscore God's concern for all creation. However, Luke only tells us the crowd's reaction and not the widow's reaction. But I am certain that the widow was happy for her restoration so that she shared the story with everyone she encountered. And her testimony would have transformed people's lives. Embodying the story of her restoration would have been the generous gift of gaze to others. In her, Jesus would have found an emissary for his message. Christian widows in northern Nigeria have also been given the gift of generous gaze. For this reason, the widows need to be given the opportunity to share the gift of such generous gaze through embodied agency.

What the concept of gaze demonstrates is that a theological appraisal of embodiment aids in the overarching discussion about how Christians mediate Jesus' transformative power that leads to social change. This study contributes to the discussion by highlighting how Christian widows become agents of social change in northern Nigeria. As I demonstrated in the study, there are articles and chapters in books on widows in northern Nigeria; however, there are no books devoted specifically to widows in northern Nigeria. Moreover, the articles and chapters on widows in northern Nigeria ignore Christian widows in northern Nigeria. Their voices are pertinent to the conversations regarding widowhood in Africa. This study provides references to the voices of Christian widows in northern Nigeria.

In general, the literature on African widows is more interested with the conventional requirements for African widows within African societies. What I mean is that the volumes on African widows focus on how widows fit within societies' established norms.[19] It is not surprising that the major interest of the literature on African widows is on issues of remarriage and property inheritance, which stems from the assumption that all African women need to be married.[20] By focusing on remarriage and property inheritance of African widows, widows within most of the literature become peripheral in studies about them. In other words, while remarriage and

---

19. Kirwen, *African Widows*; Gray and Gulliver, *Family Estate*; Evans-Pritchard, *Kinship*; Cohen, *Custom and Politics*.

20. Potash, *Widows in African Societies*, 3.

property inheritance are not bad in themselves, they have become issues used to undermine the agency of African widows. Even literature that attempt to treat widows as a central theme are also hampered by their focus on remarriage and property inheritance of African widows.[21] Considering widows' potential for agency through the purview of remarriage and property inheritance undermines widows' agency to effect social change. African societies need to embrace the notion that widows can contribute significantly towards social change.

This study does not look at widows' agency through the purview of remarriage and inheritance or limit the conversation around social expectations of African widows. Rather, I consider widows' embodied agency through theological and social science lenses. I demonstrated that widows' agency is informed by divine calling, where widows have a God-given mandate to extend Jesus' generous gaze to society. I challenged African societies to consider the positive and significant impacts widows can make towards social change. What I argue is that African societies must empower widows to become agents of social change. While some of the literature advocates for empowering widows, I suggest that empowering them *should* involve enabling widows to become agents of social change. In other words, I do not only suggest we help widows attain autonomy; rather, I suggest that African societies should position widows to use their autonomy to transform society. Failure to empower widows without positioning them to effect social change has the potential of making autonomous widows participants in the perpetuation of injustice against others. By looking at widows in a restorative manner, society empowers them towards restorative gaze where widows are charged to resist every form of oppression. As recipients of generous gaze, widows contribute positively towards changing society. Social change demands the participation of Christian widows. Society needs widows to express their gift of generous gaze that leads to social change.

In sum, empowerment is central to Christianity. Christians in northern Nigeria believe that salvation involves empowerment to serve God with their lives. And nothing "qualifies" us to honor God more than the fact that we are God's children. Christian widows persevere with tremendous confidence in God because of the indwelling Holy Spirit. I observed the flexible and adaptable nature of the workings of the Holy Spirit in the ways the two organizations I researched serve widows. Thus, the widows' plights

---

21. Potash, *Widows in African Societies*, 3. See also Mair, "African Marriage and Social Change."

require empowerment initiatives that yield to the leading of the Holy Spirit. The Holy Spirit can broaden the widow's limited vision of the world and her interactions within the world. By the Holy Spirit, widows would realize that their divine gaze requires them to share the gaze with others. Jurgen Moltmann states that the Holy Spirit helps Christians to embrace both God's presence and community with others.[22] In other words, the Holy Spirit is pertinent to empowering widows for social change.

The presence of the Holy Spirit suggests that power comes from God. Therefore, our gaze must result in a generous sharing of that power with others. By emulating Jesus' generous gaze, Christian widows become reformers and transformers of their societies. Ka Mana expresses this more succinctly when he refers to theology as formulating the type of power that seeks to reconstruct, which both integrates and accommodates others through reformation and transformation of oneself and one's society.[23] Elias K. Bongmba also underscores Ka Mana's sentiments in his examination of the theology of reconstruction.[24] Ka Mana and Bongmba's point suggest that genuine power must impact the people and institutions that inspire and guide the lives of people. The Christian widow, whose source of power is the Spirit of God, can pursue an ever-expanding role as God's agent in the world. She can leverage her God-given social status for ongoing growth and service to those within and beyond her sphere of influence.

---

22. Moltmann, *Source of Life*.
23. Dedji, "Ethical Redemption," 254–74.
24. Bongmba, "Rethinking Power."

Bibliography

Ackerman, Denise. "From Mere Existence to Tenacious Endurance." In *African Women, Religion, and Health*, edited by Isabel A. Phiri and Sarojini Nadar, 221–42. Maryknoll, NY: Orbis, 2006.
Adams, Nicholas, and Charles Elliott. "Ethnography Is Dogmatics: Making Description Central to Systematic Theology." *Scottish Journal of Theology* 53.3 (2000) 339–64.
Adamu, Theresa. *Nasarar Gwanruwa Kirista*. Jos, Nigeria: Challenge Press, 1994.
———. *Widowhood in the 21st Century: A Call from God*. Jos, Nigeria: Animation Publisher, 2012.
Adeyemo, Tokunboh, ed. *Africa Bible Commentary: A One-Volume Commentary*. Downers Grove: Zondervan, 2010.
Adogame, Afe. "African Christianities and the Politics of Development from Below." *HTS Teologiese Studies/Theological Studies* 72.4 (2016) 1–11.
———. "How God Became a Nigerian: Religious Impulse and the Unfolding of a Nation." *Journal of Contemporary African Studies* 28.4 (2010) 479–98.
Allegranti, Beatrice. *Embodied Performances: Sexuality, Gender, Bodies*. London: Palgrave Macmillan, 2011.
Alumka, Dan. *Who Is a Widow?* Abuja, Nigeria: First Impact, 2014.
Anderson, Allan. "African Indigenous Churches and Pentecostalism." *Mission Studies* 16–12, 32 (1999) 197–98.
———. "African Pentecostal Churches and Concepts of Power." Paper presented at the Africa Forum, Council of Churches for Britain and Ireland, April 1997.
Awans, Joseph Bagaiya. "An Analysis of the Objectives of ECWA Widows' School, Samaru Kataf." Master's thesis, Jos ECWA Theological Seminary, 1992.
Awolalu, J., and P. A. Dopamu. *West African Traditional Religion*. Ibadan, Nigeria: Onibonoje, 1979.
Barber, Karin. *The Anthropology of Texts, Persons and Publics: Oral and Written Culture in Africa and Beyond*. Cambridge, UK: Cambridge University Press, 2007.

Bibliography

Barz, Gregory F. *Performing Religion: Negotiating Past and Present in Kwaya Music of Tanzania*. Amsterdam: Rodopi, 2003.

Bauta, Sung. "Empowering Widows with Orality-Framed Training." *Mission Frontiers* 36.3 (2014) 10.

BBC. "Who Are Nigeria's Boko Haram Islamists?" *BBC News*, November 24, 2016. https://www.bbc.com/news/world-africa-13809501 (accessed June 30, 2018).

Bediako, Kwame. *Christianity in Africa: The Renewal of a Non-Western Religion*. Edinburgh: Edinburgh University Press, 1995.

Berger, Peter L. "Max Weber Is Alive and Well, and Living in Guatemala: The Protestant Ethic Today." *The Review of Faith and International Affairs* 8.4 (2010) 3–9.

Bernard, H. Russell. *Research Methods in Anthropology: Qualitative and Quantitative Approaches*. New York: Altamira, 2006.

Beya, Bernadette Mbuy. "Human Sexuality, Marriage, and Prostitution." In *The Will to Arise: Women, Tradition, and the Church in Africa*, edited by Mercy Amba Oduyoye and Musimbi R. A. Kanyoro, 155–81. Maryknoll, NY: Orbis, 1992.

Biddle, Tabby. "Women as Peacemakers." *HuffPost*, December 6, 2017. https://www.huffpost.com/entry/women-as-peacemakers_b_282997.

Bompani, Barbara, and Maria Frahm-Arp, eds. *Development and Politics from Below: Exploring Religious Spaces in the African State*. New York: Palgrave Macmillan, 2010.

Bonat, Deborah. "The Challenges of Widowhood." Paper presented at chapel service of ECWA Theological Seminary, Kagoro, Nigeria, April 20, 2015.

Bongmba, Elias K. "Rethinking Power in Africa: Theological Perspectives." *Religion & Theology* 11.2 (2004) 103–38.

Bruner, Jerome S. *Acts of Meaning*. Cambridge, MA: Harvard University Press, 1990.

Brusco, Elizabeth E. *The Reformation of Machismo: Evangelical Conversion and Gender in Colombia*. Austin: University of Texas Press, 1995.

Bultmann, Rudolf. *Theology of the New Testament*. Vol. 2. Translated by Kendrick Grobel. London: SCM, 1988.

Burgess, Richard. *Nigeria's Christian Revolution: The Civil War and Its Pentecostal Progeny, 1967–2004*. Carlisle:Regnum, 2008.

———. "Pentecostals and Development in Nigeria and Zambia: Community Organizing as a Response to Poverty and Violence." *PentecoStudies* 14.2 (2015) 176–204.

Buvinic, Mayra, Margaret A. Lycette, and William Paul McGreevey, eds. *Women and Poverty in the Third World*. Baltimore: The Johns Hopkins University Press, 1983.

Carson, D. A. "Reflections on Contextualization: A Critical Appraisal of Daniel Von Allmen's 'Birth of Theology.'" *East Africa Journal of Evangelical Theology* 3.1 (1984) 16–59.

CIA. "Nigeria." *CIA World Factbook*. https://www.cia.gov/the-world-factbook/countries/nigeria/.

Cochrane, John R. "Health and Uses of Religion: Recovering the Political Proper." In *Development and Politics from Below: Exploring Religious Spaces in the African State*, edited by Barbara Bompani and Maria Frahm-Arp, 175–96. New York: Palgrave Macmillan, 2010.

Cohen, Abner. *Custom and Politics in Urban Africa*. Berkeley: University of California Press, 1969.

Connor, Walker. "A Nation Is a Nation, Is a State, Is an Ethnic Group, Is a . . ." *Ethnic and Racial Studies* 1.4 (1978) 377–400.

Bibliography

Dedji, Valentine. "The Ethical Redemption of African Imaginaire: Ka Mana's Theology of Reconstruction." *Journal of Religion in Africa* 31.3 (2001) 254–74.

Denhart, R. B., and P. W. Jeffress. "Social Learning and Economic Behavior: The Process of Economic Socialization." *American Journal of Economics and Sociology* 30.2 (1971) 113–25.

Dickson, Kwesi A., and Paul Ellingworth, eds. *Biblical Revelation and African Beliefs.* Cambridge, UK: Lutterworth Press, 1969.

Duncan, Beatrice Akua. "Cocoa, Marriage, Labour and Land in Ghana: Some Matrilineal and Patrilineal Perspectives." *Africa: Journal of the International African Institute* 80.2 (2010) 301–21.

Durkheim, Emile. *The Elementary Forms of the Religious Life.* London: George Allen & Unwin, 1915.

Duze, Mustapha C., and Ismaila Z. Mohammed. "Male Knowledge, Attitudes, and Family Planning Practices in Northern Nigeria." *African Journal of Reproductive Health* 10.3 (2006) 53–65.

Dzubinski, Leanne M. "Taking on Power: Women Leaders in Evangelical Mission Organizations." *Missiology: An International Review* 44, 3 (2016) 281–95.

Edet, Rosemary N. "Christianity and African Women's Rituals." In *The Will to Arise: Women, Tradition, and the Church in Africa*, edited by Mercy Amba Oduyoye and Musimbi R. A. Kanyoro. Maryknoll, NY: Orbis, 1992.

Ela, Jean-Marc. *African Cry.* Maryknoll, NY: Orbis, 1986.

———. *My Faith as an African.* Eugene, OR: Wipf & Stock, 2009.

Ellis, Stephen T. "Development and Invisible Worlds." In *Development and Politics from Below: Exploring Religious Spaces in the African State*, edited by Barbara Bompani and Maria Frahm-Arp, 23–39. New York: Palgrave Macmillan, 2010.

Ellis, Stephen T., and Gerrie Ter Haar. *Worlds of Power: Religious Thought and Political Practice in Africa.* New York: Oxford University Press, 2004.

Eisenstadt, Shmuel Noah. "Social Change and Modernization in African Societies South of the Sahara." *Cahiers d'études africaines* 5.19 (1965) 453–71.

Enemo, Ifeoma. "Widowhood and Property Inheritance under Customary Law." In *Essays in Contemporary Legal Issues*, edited by C. E. Emole et al., 290–311. Enugu, Nigeria: Auto-Century, 1996.

Evans-Pritchard, E. E. *Kinship and Marriage Among the Nuer.* Oxford: Clarendon, 1969.

Federal Republic of Nigeria. "Constitution of the Federal Republic of Nigeria 1999." http://www.nigeria-law.org/ConstitutionOfTheFederalRepublicOfNigeria.htm.

———. "Marriage Act, chapter 218." http://www.nigeria-law.org/Marriage%20Act.htm.

Frank, Barbara. "Gendered Ritual Dualism in a Patrilineal Society: Opposition and Complementarity in Kulere Fertility Cults." *Africa: Journal of the International African Institute* 74.2 (2004) 217–40.

Freeman, Dena. "The Pentecostal Ethic and the Spirit of Development." In *Pentecostalism and Development: Churches, NGOs, and Social Change in Africa*, edited by D. Freeman, 1–40. Basingstoke, UK: Palgrave Macmillan, 2012.

Gannep, Arnold van. *Rites of Passage.* Translated by M. B. Vizedom and G. L. Caffee. 1909. Reprint, Chicago: University of Chicago Press, 1960.

Ganusah, Rebecca. "The Church and Development: A Ghanaian Experience." *Studies In World Christianity & Interreligious Relations* 48.1 (2014) 203–18.

Garba, Gladys K. "Building Women's Capacity for Peace Building in Nigeria." *Review of History and Political Science* 4.1 (2016) 31–46.

Bibliography

Getui, Mary N., and Emmanuel A. Obeng, eds. *Theology of Reconstruction: Exploratory Articles*. Nairobi, Kenya: Acton, 1999.

Giddens, Anthony. *The Constitution of Society: Outline of the Theory of Structuration*. Cambridge, UK: Polity, 1984.

Gifford, Paul. *African Christianity: Its Public Role*. Bloomington, IN: Indiana University Press, 1998.

———. *Christianity, Development and Modernity in Africa*. Oxford: Oxford University Press, 2016.

———. *Ghana's New Christianity: Pentecostalism in a Globalizing African Economy*. Bloomington, IN: Indiana University Press, 2004.

Green, Joel B. *The Gospel of Luke*. The New International Commentary on the New Testament. Grand Rapids: Eerdmans, 1997.

Gray, Robert F., and Philip Gulliver, eds. *The Family Estate in Africa*. Boston: Boston University Press, 1964.

The Guardian. "Nigeria becomes Africa's Largest Economy." *The Guardian Datablog*, April 7, 2014. https://www.theguardian.com/global-development/datablog/2014/apr/07/nigeria-becomes-africa-largest-economy-get-data.

Hadisi, Mwana. "Exploring the Performance, Semantic, and Cognitive Dimensions of Orality." *Missiology* 40.4 (2012) 443–53.

Harrison, Beverly. *Making the Connection: Essays in Feminist Social Ethics*. Boston: Beacon, 1985.

Hastings, Adrian, ed. *A World History of Christianity*. Grand Rapids: Eerdmans, 1999.

Hiebert, Paul. "Critical Contextualization." *International Bulletin of Missionary Research* 11.3 (1987) 104–11.

Hock, Klaus, ed. *The Power of Interpretation: Imagined Authenticity—Appropriated Identity*. Conflicting Discourses on New Forms of African Christianity. Wiesbaden, Germany: Harrassowitz, 2016.

Holmes, Peter. *Nigeria: Giant of Africa*. Lagos, Nigeria: National Oil and Chemical Marketing Co., 1987.

Horton, R. "African Conversion." *Africa* 41.2 (1971) 85–108.

Hudson, Valerie M., and Hilary Matfess. "In Plain Sight: The Neglected Linkage between Brideprice and Violent Conflict." *International Security* 42.1 (2017) 7–40.

Huntington, Samuel P. *Political Order in Changing Societies*. New Haven: Yale University Press, 1968.

Ibeabuchi, Apollos Oziogu. "Body Painting Art in Nigeria." *Vanguard*, July 21, 2011. https://www.vanguardngr.com/2011/07/body-painting-art-in-nigeria/.

Ibhawoh, Bonny. *Between Culture and Constitution: The Cultural Legitimacy of Human Rights in Nigeria*. Copenhagen: Danish Center for Human Rights, 1999.

Idowu, Bolaji. *African Traditional Religion: A Definition*. Maryknoll, NY: Orbis, 1973.

———. *Oludumare: God in Yoruba Belief*. London: Longman, 1962.

Iheanacho, Ngozi N. "The Alienation of Nigerian Women in Widowhood." *The Journal of Pan African Studies* 8.7 (2015) 19–40.

Ijiomah, C. "African Philosophy's Contribution to the Dialogue on Reality Issues." *Sankofa: Journal of the Humanities* 3.1 (2005) 81–90.

Inazu, John. "No Future without (Personal) Forgiveness: Reexamining the Role of Forgiveness in Transnational Justice." *Human Rights Review* 10.3 (2009) 309–26.

Institute of Medicine. *Insuring America's Health: Principles and Recommendations*. Washington, DC: The National Academies, 2004.

Bibliography

Inuwa, Jummai. *ECWA Widow's School Happenings*. Kaduna, Nigeria: ECWA, 2014.
Iwobi, Andrew Ubaka. "No Cause for Merriment: The Position of Widows under Nigerian Law." *Canadian Journal of Women & The Law* 20.1(2008) 37–86.
Janfa, Comfort R. *The Mystery of Success in Widowhood*. Jos, Nigeria: Albishir, 2010.
Johnson, Elizabeth A. *She Who Is: The Mystery of God in Feminist Theological Discourse*. New York: Crossroad, 1992.
Kato, Byang H. *Theological Pitfalls in Africa*. Kisumu, Kenya: Evangel, 1975.
Katongole, Emmanuel. *A Future for Africa: Critical Essays in Christian Social Imagination*. Scranton, PA: University of Scranton Press, 2005.
———. *The Sacrifice of Africa: A Political Theology for Africa*. Grand Rapids: Eerdmans, 2011.
Kalmin, Richard. "Levirate Law." In *Anchor Bible Dictionary*, edited by David Freeman, 4:296. New York: Doubleday, 1992.
Kalu, Ogbu. *African Pentecostalism: An Introduction*. Oxford: Oxford University Press, 2008.
Kanu, Ikechukwu A. "The Dimensions of African Cosmology." *Filosofia Theoretica: Journal of African Philosophy, Culture and Religion* 2.2 (2013) 537–39.
Karam, Azza. "The Role of Religious Actors in Implementing the UN's Sustainable Goals." *The Ecumenical Review* 38.4 (2016) 365–77.
Khan, Aslam, and Lawan Cheri. "An Examination of Poverty as the Foundation of Crisis in Northern Nigeria." *Insights on Africa* 8.1 (2016) 59–71.
Kirwen, Michael. *African Widows: An Empirical Study of the Problems of Adapting Western Christian Teachings on Marriage to the Leviratic Custom for the Care of Widows in Four Rural African Societies*. Maryknoll, NY: Orbis, 1979.
Kozieł, Patrycia. "Hausa Women's Rights and Changing the Perception of Gender in Northern Nigeria." *Literature and Culture Studies* (2017) 217–29.
Kuper, Ayelet, Lorelei Lingard, and Wendy Levinson. "Critically Appraising Qualitative Research." *British Medical Journal* 337 (2008) 1035.
Lageer, Eileen. *New Life for All: True Accounts of In-Depth Evangelism in West Africa*. Chicago: Moody, 1969.
Leach, Cindy. "Orality and Learning Theories." *Text Technologies*, October 3, 2010. https://blogs.ubc.ca/etec540sept10/2010/10/03/orality-and-learning-theories/.
Levine, N. E., and Walter H. Sangree. "Conclusion: Asian and African Systems of Polyandry." *Journal of Comparative Family Studies* 11.3 (1980) 385–410.
Locka, Christian. "Cameroon Uses Witchcraft to Fight Boko Haram." *USA Today*, January 12, 2017. https://www.usatoday.com/story/news/world/2017/01/12/cameroon-uses-witchcraft-fight-boko-haram/96480570/.
Luz, Ulrich. *Matthew 8–20: A Commentary*. Edited by Helmut Koester, translated by James E. Crouch. Minneapolis: Fortress, 2001.
Madinger, Charles. "A Literate's Guide to the Oral Galaxy." *Orality Journal* 2.2 (2013) 12–40.
———. *Widows of Ambam Kaninkon*. Jos, Nigeria: self-published, 2007.
Macionis, John J., and Linda M. Gerber. *Sociology*. Toronto: Pearson, 2011.
Mair, Lucy P. "African Marriage and Social Change." In *Survey of African Marriage and Family Life*, edited by A. Philips, 1–171. London: Oxford University Press, 1953.
Marshall, Ruth. *Political Spiritualities: The Pentecostal Revolution in Nigeria*. Chicago: University of Chicago Press, 2009.

Bibliography

Martin, David. "Pentecostalism: An Alternative Form of Modernity and Modernization?" In *Global Pentecostalism in the 21st Century*, edited by Robert. W. Hefner, 37–62. Bloomington, IN: Indiana University Press, 2013.

———. *Pentecostalism: The World Their Parish*. Oxford: Blackwell, 2002.

Mbiti, John. *African Religions and Philosophy*. London: Heinemann, 1990.

Metz, Helen Chapin. "Nigeria: A Country Study—The Slave Trade." *Library of Congress Country Studies*. http://countrystudies.us/nigeria/7.htm.

McMillan, Uri. *Embodied Avatars: Genealogies of Black Feminist Art and Performance*. New York: New York University Press, 2015.

Merleau-Ponty, Maurice. *Phenomenology of Perception*. Translated by Donald A. Landes. 1945. Reprint, London: Routledge, 2012.

Meyer, Birgit. "Going and Making Public: Pentecostalism as Public Religion in Ghana." In *Christianity and Public Culture in Africa*, edited by Harri Englund, 149–66. Athens, OH: Ohio University Press, 2011.

Miller, D. E., and T. Yamamori. *Global Pentecostalism: The New Face of Christian Social Engagement*. Berkeley: University of California Press, 2007.

Moltmann, Jurgen. *The Source of Life: The Holy Spirit and the Theology of Life*. Minneapolis: Fortress, 1997.

Morris, Leon. *Luke*. Tyndale New Testament Commentaries. Grand Rapids: Eerdmans, 1990.

Motty, Bauta D. *Indigenous Christian Disciple-Making*. Jos, Nigeria: ECWA, 2013.

Mudimbe, V. Y. *Africa's Dependence and the Remedies*. Paris: Berger-Levrault, 1980.

———. *The Invention of Africa: Gnosis, Philosophy, and the Order of Knowledge*. Bloomington, IN: Indiana University Press, 1988.

Mugambi, J. N. K. *From Liberation to Reconstruction: African Christian Theology after the Cold War*. Nairobi, Kenya: East African Educational, 1995.

Mustapha, R. "Ethnicity and the Politics of Democratization in Nigeria." In *Ethnicity & Democracy in Africa*, edited by B. Berman, D. Eyoh, and W. Kymlicka, 257–75. Oxford: James Currey, 2004.

Mutume, Gumisai. "African Women Battle for Equality." *Africa Renewal Online*, July 2005. http://www.un.org/africarenewal/magazine/july-2005/african-women-battle-equality.

Myers, Bryant. *Walking with the Poor: Principles and Practices of Transformational Development*. Maryknoll, NY: Orbis, 1999.

Ngbea, Gabriel T., and Hilary C. Achunike. "Poverty in Northern Nigeria." *Asian Journal of Humanities and Social Studies* 2.2 (April 2014). http://ajouronline.com/index.php?journal=AJHSS&page=article&op=view&path%5B%5D=1018.

Oduyoye, Mercy Amba. *Daughters of Anowa: African Women and Patriarchy*. Maryknoll, NY: Orbis, 1995.

———. "Women and Ritual in Africa." In *The Will to Arise: Women, Tradition, and the Church in Africa*, edited by Mercy Amba Oduyoye and Musimbi R. A. Kanyoro, 9–24. Maryknoll, NY: Orbis, 1992.

Ogedegbe, Bosede Gladys. "Christian Religion as Tool for Women Empowerment in Nigeria." *Journal of Emerging Trends in Educational Research and Policy Studies* 6.3 (2015) 245–49.

Ogoloma, Fineface I., and Wilfred I. Ukpere. "The Role of Women in Peacemaking, Conflict and Rehabilitation Management in Elele, Ikwerre Local Government of

Bibliography

Rivers State, Nigeria." *African Journal of Business Management* 5.33 (2011) 12,711–14.

Ojo, Matthew A. "The Growth of Charismatic Movements in Northern Nigeria." *Ogbomosho Journal of Theology* 13.2 (2008) 83–121.

Okesson, Gregg A. "Christian Witness to Institutions: Public Missiology and Power." *Missiology: An International Review* 44.2 (2016) 142–54.

Okoye, Pat U. *Widowhood: A Natural or Cultural Tragedy*. Enugu, Nigeria: Nucik, 1995.

Olupona, Jacob. *African Traditional Religions in Contemporary Society*. St. Paul, MN: Paragon, 1991.

Omoregbe, O. O. "Perspectives on Urban and Rural Women." In *Women in Law*, edited by Akintunde O. Obilade, 160–62. Lagos: Southern University Law Centre and Faculty of Law, 1993.

Ong, Walter. *Orality and Literacy: The Technologizing of the Word*. London: Methuen, 1982.

Orobator, Agbonkhianmeghe E. *Theology Brewed in an African Pot*. Maryknoll, NY: Orbis, 2009

Osei-Bonsu, Joseph. *The Inculturation of Christianity in Africa*. Frankfurt: Peter Lang, 2005.

Otite, O. "Nigeria's Identifiable Ethnic Groups." *Online Nigeria*. https://www.onlinenigeria.com/tribes/tribes.php.

Owen, Margaret. "Widows in Third World Nations." *Encyclopedia of Death and Dying*. http://www.deathreference.com/Vi-Z/Widows-in-Third-World-Nations.html.

Parsitau, Damaris. "Arise, Oh Ye Daughters of Faith: Women, Pentecostalism, and Public Culture in Kenya." In *Christianity and Public Culture in Africa*, edited by Harri Englund, 131–48. Athens, OH: Ohio University Press, 2011.

Pereira, Charmaine, and Jibrin Ibrahim. "On the Bodies of Women: The Common Ground between Islam and Christianity." *Third World Quarterly* 31.6 (2010) 921–37.

Phiri, Isabel A., and Sarojini Nadar, eds. *African Women, Religion, and Health*. Maryknoll, NY: Orbis, 2006.

Pobee, John. *Toward an African Theology*. Nashville: Abingdon, 1979.

Potash, Betty, ed. *Widows in African Societies*. Stanford, CA: Stanford University Press, 1986.

Quarcoopome, T. N. *West African Traditional Religion*. Ibadan, Nigeria: African Universities Press, 1987.

Rokoczy, Susan. "Women and Peacemaking: The Challenge of a Non-Violent Life." In *African Women, Religion, and Health*, edited by Isabel A. Phiri and Sarojini Nadar, 187–207. Maryknoll, NY: Orbis, 2006.

Rosenblatt, Paul C., and Busisiwe Catherine Nkosi. "South African Zulu Widows in a Time of Poverty and Social Change." *Death Studies* 31.1 (2007) 67–85.

Rotimi, Adewale. "Paradox of 'Progress': The Role of Western Education in the Transformation of the Family in Nigeria." *Anthropologist* 7.2 (2005) 137–47.

Rupp, Nicole, Peter Breunig, and Stephanie Kahlheber. "Exploring the Nok Enigma." *Antiquity* 82.316 (June 2008). http://www.antiquity.ac.uk/projgall/kahlheber316/.

Sangree, Walter H. "The Persistence of Polyandry in Irigwe, Nigeria." *Journal of Comparative Family Studies* 11.3 (1980) 335–43.

———. "Tribal Ritual, Leadership and the Mortality Rate in Irigwe, Northern Nigeria." *Southwestern Journal of Anthropology* 26 (1970) 32–39.

Bibliography

Sanneh, Lamin. *Translating the Message: The Missionary Impact on Culture.* Maryknoll, NY: Orbis, 1989.

Schildkrout, Enid. "Widows in Hausa Society: Ritual Phase or Social Status?" In *Widows in African Societies,* edited by Betty Potash, 131–52. Stanford: Stanford University Press, 1986.

Schulz, Dorothea E. "Remaking Society from Within: Extraversion and the Social Forms of Female Muslim Activism in Urban Mali." In *Development and Politics from Below: Exploring Religious Spaces in the African State,* edited by Barbara Bompani and Maria Frahm-Arp, 74–98. New York: Palgrave Macmillan, 2010.

Shaw, T. M. *Towards A Political Economy of Africa: The Dialectics of Dependence.* New York: St. Martin's, 1985.

Sigurdson, Ola. *Heavenly Bodies: Incarnation, the Gaze, and Embodiment in Christian Theology.* Grand Rapids: Eerdmans, 2016.

Spradley, James P. *Participant Observation.* Fort Worth, TX: Harcourt College, 1980.

Starkweather, Katie. "A Preliminary Survey of Lesser-Known Polyandrous Societies." *Nebraska Anthropologist* 50 (2009) 17–35.

Stanford Encyclopedia of Philosophy. "Social Institutions." https://plato.stanford.edu/entries/social-institutions/.

Stone, Linda. *Kinship and Gender: An Introduction.* Boulder, CO: Westview, 2013.

Sturken, Marita, and Lisa Cartwright. *Practices of Looking: An Introduction to Visual Culture.* Oxford: Oxford University Press, 2001.

Taidi, Tabitha. *The Widow and the Challenges of Widowhood.* Minna, Nigeria: Self-published, n.d.

Tanabe, Rosie. "African Philosophy." *New World Encyclopedia.* http://www.newworldencyclopedia.org/p/index.php?title=African_philosophy&oldid=99403.

Thurston, Alexander. *Boko Haram: The History of an African Jihadist Movement.* Princeton: Princeton University Press, 2017.

Turaki, Yusufu. *Tainted Legacy: Islam, Colonialism and Slavery in Northern Nigeria.* McLean, VA: Isaac, 2010.

Turner, Victor. *The Ritual Process: Structure and Anti-Structure.* New York: Aldine, 1995.

Turner, Jonathan. *The Institutional Order.* New York: Longman, 1997.

Tutu, Desmond. *No Future without Forgiveness.* New York: Doubleday, 2000.

Tylor, Edward B. *Religion in Primitive Culture.* New York: Harper Torchbooks, 1958.

United Nations. "1966 International Covenant on Economic, Social and Cultural Rights." https://www.ohchr.org/en/professionalinterest/pages/cescr.aspx.

United States Women's Bureau. "The United Nations Decade for Women, 1976–1985." https://archive.org/details/unitednationsdecoounit.

Udoh, Enyi Ben. *Guest Christology: An Interpretive View of the Christological Problem in Africa.* Frankfurt: Lang, 1988.

Urbaniak, Jakub. "Between the Christ of Deep Incarnation and the African Jesus of Tinyiko Maluleke: An Improvised Dialogue." *Modern Theology* 34.2 (2018) 177–205.

USAID. "The Key Role of Faith-Based Organizations in Strengthening Human Resources for Health." *USAID / Capacity Plus.* http://www.capacityplus.org/sites/intrah.civicactions.net/files/resources/FBO_overview.pdf.

Uzukwu, Elochukwu E. *A Listening Church: Autonomy and Communion in the African Church.* Eugene, OR: Wipf and Stock, 1996.

Bibliography

Vaidyanathan, B. "Religious Resources or Differential Returns? Early Religious Socialization and Declining Attendance in Emerging Adulthood." *Journal for the Scientific Study of Religion* 50.2 (2011) 366–87.

The Veritas Forum. "Learning to Live with Our Enemies." *YouTube*, September 17, 2017. https://www.youtube.com/watch?v=CqTpmGdXjfk.

Villa-Vicencio, Charles. *A Theology of Reconstruction: Nation-Building and Human Rights.* Cambridge, UK: Cambridge University Press, 1992.

Volf, Miroslav. *Exclusion and Embrace: A Theological Exploration of Identity, Otherness, and Reconciliation.* Nashville: Abingdon, 1996.

Wariboko, Nimi. "Pentecostalism in Africa." *Oxford Research Encyclopedia of African History*, October 26, 2017. http://africanhistory.oxfordre.com/view/10.1093/acrefore/9780190277734.001.0001/acrefore-9780190277734-e-120.

Wundengba, Charles. "The Role of the 21st-Century Woman in Peacebuilding." May 2017. https://wundef.com/the-role-of-the-21st-century-woman-in-peacebuilding/.

Zaggi, Hassan. "Nigeria: Involving Women in Peace Building Process." *AllAfrica*, October 11, 2014. http://allafrica.com/stories/201410130978.html.

Index

Adamu, Theresa, 3, 4, 6, 7, 102
Adogame, Afe, 53–54, 112
African Cosmology, 37–41, 45–46, 55
African Traditional Religion (ATR), 37, 92
Agency, x, 4, 7, 8, 10, 11–13, 15–16, 20, 24–31, 36, 46, 49, 52–56, 58–65, 67, 69–70, 72–73, 75, 78–80, 82–86, 88–99, 101–10, 113, 115–25, 127–30, 132–35, 139–42, 145–47
Anthropological, Anthropologist(s), 6, 9–10, 55, 60, 91, 121–22
Appropriating, Appropriation(s), 7, 93, 110
Bible, Biblical, 9, 16, 18–19, 41, 53, 65–66, 68–70, 76, 81–83, 85, 93–98, 103, 109, 112, 116, 123, 127, 135, 140
Christian Widow(s)/Widow(s), ix-29, 31–32, 35–36, 39–61, 63–110, 113–47
Christianity, Christians, ix, x, 7, 9–14, 19–20, 22, 25, 27–34, 37, 39–40, 46, 49, 51, 53–56, 59, 66–67, 70, 72, 74–75, 78–80, 84–86, 89, 91–94, 96, 99–100, 102, 110–11, 114, 116, 119–22, 125, 127, 129, 137, 139–40, 143, 145–48

Christology, 111–13, 118, 124
Church, Churches, xi, xii, 3, 22, 25, 27, 53–54, 59, 70, 85–86, 88–92, 95, 99–100, 103–8, 119, 127, 134, 139
Death(s), Dead, 3, 4, 15, 18, 27, 30, 38, 40–41, 43–44, 46, 48–51, 56, 62–63, 68, 78, 85, 104, 114–16, 118, 121, 126, 129, 131–32, 135–36, 138, 143
Development, ix, xii, 5, 8, 11–13, 52–54, 61, 64–66, 72, 74–77, 79, 86–87, 89–95, 100, 102, 109–10, 114, 120–22, 140
Embody, Embodied, Embodiment, x, 4–13, 24–25, 27, 32, 49, 74, 77, 89, 97, 109–25, 127–29, 131–42, 145–47
ECWA, xiii, 16–17, 20, 23, 89, 94
Economy, Economic, 4, 8, 10, 12, 15, 23, 25, 28, 33, 35, 41–42, 44, 54, 56, 58–61, 64–65, 71–75, 78, 82–83, 85, 87, 99–100, 105, 107, 122
Education, Educate, 3, 15, 17–20, 23, 53, 56–57, 67, 69, 72–75, 82, 87, 90, 92–94, 107–8, 135
Ela, Jean-Marc, 66–67, 70

Index

Empower(s), Empowering, Empowerment, 3, 8, 10, 13–14, 16–18, 20–21, 23–25, 29, 54–55, 70, 73, 75, 80–82, 84–86, 103, 141–43, 145, 147–48

EWS, xiii, 16–18, 20–22, 48, 53, 60, 63, 65, 67, 69, 72–75, 78, 80–81, 88–89, 92–94, 97, 101, 105, 107–8, 114, 116, 118, 121, 125, 127, 130, 132, 134

Faith, xii, 3–4, 10–12, 14, 18, 22, 25, 31, 36, 54–55, 58–59, 61, 64–67, 69, 70–85, 88, 91–94, 96, 102–3, 106, 109–10, 117, 119–20, 122, 134, 138, 140

Feminist Theologians, 13, 27–28, 39, 41, 46, 55, 61–62, 113, 118–20, 142

GAWON, xiii, 16, 18–22, 54, 57, 61, 65, 67, 72–73, 78, 80, 89, 114, 121, 130

Gaze, 10, 13, 114, 117, 129, 142–48

Gender, Gender roles, 10, 15, 56

Gifford, Paul, 52–54, 72, 74, 90–91, 99, 102, 104, 106

Holistic, Holism, xii, 5, 7–8, 13, 29, 72, 85–86, 88–95, 109, 114, 118, 120–23, 140

Holy Spirit, 96–97, 100, 103 110, 142, 147–48

Incarnation, 10, 13, 110–14, 116, 118–20, 123–29, 131, 133–34, 136–40, 142–43

Inculturation, ix, 5, 8–10, 13, 114, 120, 124, 128

Institutions, Institutional, x-xii, 4, 7, 10, 12, 16, 24–27, 54, 84–96, 98, 100–106, 108–9, 119, 141–42

Land, 2–4, 15, 32, 56, 58, 73, 104

Liminal Phase, 6, 49–51, 131–32, 142

Mainline Church(es), 8, 53, 94, 96–97, 102, 104, 106, 108

Maltreatment, 2, 27, 35, 52, 57, 68, 118, 121, 136

Marketable Skills, 15, 53, 57, 69, 72, 74–75

Marginalization, Marginality, x, 15–16, 20, 29, 36, 39, 41, 44, 54, 55, 78, 82, 115–16, 122, 134

Mediate(s), Mediating, Mediated, 10, 12–13, 59, 98, 110, 113–18, 120, 123–24, 126, 128–29, 131, 133–34, 136, 137, 139–40, 146

Mothers, 5, 6, 26, 56, 58, 60–61, 64, 68, 83

Mourning Ritual(s), Rituals, xii, 6–10, 12–13, 30–31, 37, 39, 42–43, 46–52, 56, 60, 63, 97, 110, 113–18, 120, 123–25, 127, 129, 131, 133–34, 136–38, 140–41

Muslim, Islam(ic), 19–21, 25, 27, 29, 33, 36–37, 54, 77, 81–82, 92, 99

NGOs, ix, x, 2, 4, 19–20, 22, 25, 52, 88–89

Northern Nigeria, ix, xi-9, 11–12, 14–16, 18, 20–23, 25–37, 39, 41–56, 58–65, 67, 70–72, 74–75, 77–79, 81–93, 95–96, 98–103, 105, 108, 110, 114–15, 117, 123–26, 128–31, 133–47

Oral, 123, 126, 128

Patriarchy, Patriarchal, x, 8, 41, 46, 70, 107

Patrimonialism, 90, 99

Pentecostalism, Pentecostal, 7, 8, 12, 52–53, 72, 85–86, 95, 97–109, 120

Political, Politics, 10–11, 31–32, 44, 53, 59, 66–67, 76–77, 81–82, 87, 90, 98–99, 136–37

Power, Powerlessness, ix, x, 3, 8, 10, 12–15, 27–28, 36, 38, 39, 41, 42–43, 45, 55, 82, 87, 97–98, 101, 104, 106, 108, 110, 113–14, 120, 123–26, 128–29, 131, 133–34, 136–42, 144, 146, 148

Poverty, ix, x, 31, 34–36, 57, 72–73, 98–99, 119

Pray, Prayer(ful), xii, 3, 59, 65, 67–68, 70, 72, 78, 86, 127, 134, 139

Private, 7–8, 10, 77

Public, 7–9, 66, 77, 82, 87, 99–100, 103–4, 107

Religion, Religious, xi-xiii, 4–7, 10–12, 15–16, 19, 21, 24–26, 28–33, 35–37, 39–49, 51–56, 56, 58–70, 73, 76–77, 82–84, 87–92, 98–101, 104–7, 111, 116, 118, 122, 126, 129, 135, 141–43

Index

Rite of Passage, Rites, 6, 12, 31, 37, 46, 48–49, 50–52, 56, 132, 134, 141
Schulz, Dorothea E, 77–80, 82
Sigurdson, Ola, 13, 110–11, 113–14, 116–18, 120, 124, 143–46
Social, Sociology, xi, 4, 7, 10–12, 14–16, 18, 21, 23–26, 28, 36–37, 40–41, 49, 52, 54, 56, 58–61, 63–65, 68–69, 71, 75–79, 82–89, 91, 97–98, 100–101, 105, 107, 110, 119, 121–26, 129, 135, 139, 147–48
Social Change, 4–12, 14, 16, 25–28, 31, 35–36, 46, 49, 51–54, 56, 58, 60–61, 64–80, 82–84, 93–97, 100–105, 108–9, 113–16, 118, 120–21, 123, 125, 128–29, 132–33, 135, 137–42, 146–47

Social Sciences, 5, 10, 11, 26, 51, 86, 141, 147
Status(es), 10, 12, 15–16, 28, 58, 60–63, 83, 107, 114, 121, 148
Symbol(ized), Symbolism, 6, 69, 97, 127, 130–31
Theology, Theological, ix, xii, 3–7, 9–11, 13–14, 21, 26–28, 49, 51–52, 56, 66, 70, 76, 84, 87, 91, 95–99, 102, 106, 109–13, 117, 119–20, 123, 129, 141–43, 146–48
Victorious, 102–3, 108–9, 131
Voice(s), 78, 80–83, 146
Volf, 75–80, 82
Witchcraft, 45–47, 97
Wives, 5, 6, 26, 41, 56, 58, 60–61, 63–64, 68, 83

Made in the USA
Coppell, TX
16 September 2022